PRAISE for *The Literacy Crisis*

This is the clearest argument for the absolute necessity of engaging children in literate activity—reading and writing—since Frank Smith's *Understanding Reading* was published 25 years ago. McQuillan carefully analyzes a wide variety of research to show how commonly observed effects are narrowly interpreted and misinterpreted by authors seemingly blinded by their existing biases toward particular views of how children learn to read. He builds a powerful case for continuing to refine and improve modern literacy instruction by enhancing all children's access to appropriate, engaging texts but argues persuasively that it is unequal access that produces the inequitable literacy outcomes that bedevil our schools and society. Addressing this inequity of access would truly represent an education reform initiative based in reliable, replicable research.

—**Dick Allington,** author of *No Quick Fix: Rethinking Literacy Programs in America's Elementary Schools*

Are you disturbed by endless claims about the "crisis" in beginning reading and the need to teach sounds and skills to solve it? Want a keenly argued, informed answer to these claims? Want a solidly researched alternative vision of what genuinely counts in successful reading instruction? Want "real solutions"? Then read this book!

—**Gerald Coles,** author of *The Learning Mystique: A Critical Look at Learning Disabilities*

In this book Jeff McQuillan provides the hard, statistical evidence critics of literature-based approaches to teaching reading have been demanding. He debunks studies that purport to show the superiority of phonics-based approaches to teaching reading, and argues that access to interesting books is the key to reading success.

—**David and Yvonne Freeman,** authors of *Between Worlds: Access to Second Language Acquisition*

[McQuillan's book] is without question one of the most important books on literacy ever written. It represents a major breakthrough in our understanding of the "literacy crisis."

—**Stephen Krashen,** author of *Every Person a Reader: An Alternative to the California Task Force on Reading*

Through careful analysis of current research, McQuillan calls into question the current overfocus on isolated skills and phonics and demonstrates that access to print and the amount of reading students do are the best predictors of reading achievement. As knowledgeable teachers, we must heed his findings and provide students with engaging materials, well-stocked libraries and lots of opportunity.

—**Regie Routman,** author of *Literacy at the Crossroads: Crucial Talk About Reading, Writing, and Other Teaching Dilemmas*

If we take the *Star Wars* trilogy as a metaphor for the struggle over literacy in this country, The Reading Excellence Act, the Texas and California Legislative fiats, and the new phonically rich basals represent the Empire Striking Back. With this book, Jeff McQuillan announces the Return of the Jedi. The force is with him.

—**Patrick Shannon**, author of *Reading Poverty*

This book is a "must-have" resource for any administrator, especially those who are challenged with misguided and misinformed demands from the public sector. Research citations and rebuttals are worth the price of admission to this publication.

—**Judie Thelen**, Past-President of the International Reading Association, President of Allegany County (MD) Board of Education

McQuillan offers all the evidence needed to stop the silly reading wars, if the generals will only READ IT. To paraphrase that campaign slogan: "It's the print environment, stupid!" That is, the more books, the higher the scores; fewer books, lower scores. Every school board member voting on a library issue should be forced to read this book before casting a vote.

—**Jim Trelease**, author of *The Read Aloud Handbook*

By carefully analyzing one research study after another, McQuillan demolishes some popular myths about literacy education, including the myth that whole language teaching has caused declining test scores, and the myth that intensive, systematic phonics is the answer to improving children's reading. Instead, McQuillan demonstrates that what may be THE key factor in reading achievement is not the teaching method, but ready access to books that children will love—and, of course, the time and opportunity to read them. This book should be required reading for everyone who has the opportunity to affect public and school policy: parents, community members, educators, and certainly political officeholders.

—**Constance Weaver**, author of *Reading Process and Practice: From Socio-Psycholinguistics to Whole Language, Second Edition*

Three cheers for Jeff McQuillan! For presenting an impressive array of evidence to debunk the myths that kids can't read today, that dyslexia is rampant, and that whole-language advocates deny the importance of research. This powerful, important book demolishes the claims, so prevalent today, that phonemic awareness and phonics instruction are central to learning to read, and shows that simple ingredients like time spent reading and quality libraries are what most help children become literate.

—**Sandra Wilde**, author of *What's a Schwa Sound Anyway? A Holistic Guide to Phonetics, Phonics, and Spelling*

The Literacy
CRISIS

The Literacy
CRISIS

FALSE CLAIMS, REAL SOLUTIONS

JEFF MCQUILLAN
California State University, Fullerton

HEINEMANN
Portsmouth, NH

Heinemann
A division of Reed Elsevier Inc.
361 Hanover Street
Portsmouth, NH 03801–3912
http://www.heinemann.com

Offices and agents throughout the world

Library of Congress Cataloging-in-Publication Data
McQuillan, Jeff.
    The literacy crisis : false claims, real solutions / Jeff McQuillan.
        p.   cm.
    Includes bibliographical references and index.
    ISBN 0-325-00063-8
    1. Reading—United States.   2. Literacy—United States.
    3. Language acquisition—United States.   4. Children—United States—
Books and reading.   5. Eye—Movements.   I. Title.
LB1050.2.M378   1998
428.4—DC21   98–17263
                                                                             CIP

Editor: Lois Bridges
Production: Abigail M. Heim
Cover art and design: Monty Lewis Design
Manufacturing: Courtney Ordway

Printed in the United States of America on acid-free paper

02   01   00   99   98   DA   2   3   4   5

To my parents,
Patrick and Mary McQuillan,
for always letting me go to the library
and for their unwavering trust and love

Contents

Acknowledgments

I wish to acknowledge and thank the following people for their help in writing this book: Robert Rueda, Edward Finegan, Patrick Shannon, and Connie Weaver, who shared their helpful comments on early drafts of the manuscript; Lois Bridges, who has proven to be the most inspiring, courageous, and hardworking editor any author could ask for; the entire staff and production crew at Heinemann, who made an extraordinary effort in getting this book into print; and my entire family, for their support and encouragement. Special thanks to Stephen Krashen, whose contributions to the ideas and form of this book are too numerous to describe. Most importantly, I wish to thank Lucy Tse, who discussed with me every idea, read every word, edited every page, and guided me through every revision, both intellectually and emotionally.

1

What Isn't Wrong with Reading: Seven Myths about Literacy in the United States

The simple truth is that the American public school system is slowly crippling the country by destroying the brains of its youngest citizens. . . America is literally losing its brains.
—SAMUEL BLUMENFELD (1995, P. 196)

Reading failure is epidemic. Declining test scores in reading have been noted in many states, most visibly in California, where the inability of children to read, spell, and write well has become a matter of widespread concern.
—ORTON DYSLEXIA SOCIETY (1997, P. 2)

We are turning into a nation of illiterates.
—STEPHEN PINKER (MCGUINNESS, 1997, P. IX)

Serious problems exist with reading achievement in many United States schools. Teachers are frustrated, parents puzzled, and children themselves discouraged over low reading proficiency. I have talked with teachers who tell me of such difficulties at all levels, and I witnessed them with my own eyes both when I worked as a public school teacher and when I visit schools today.

Yet in the midst of media coverage of our (latest) "literacy crisis," we should be very clear about what is and is *not* failing in our schools. Ironically, a great deal of the accepted wisdom about how United States students are performing academically is, in fact, false, which makes getting at the real problems our children face all the more difficult. The best evidence we have on the reading crisis is quite sobering: No crisis exists *on average* in United States reading, at least not of the sort reflected by the quotes above. However, other serious problems related to literacy are routinely ignored. If we are to understand how best to help those who truly need it, we must first determine what isn't true about the current status of reading achievement in America. Below are what I consider to be seven of the most prevalent—and damaging—myths about literacy achievement in the United States. Some of these have been more fully discussed by researchers elsewhere (see especially Berliner & Biddle, 1995; and Bracey, 1997a).

Myth 1: Reading Achievement in the United States Has Declined in the Past Twenty-five Years

What is striking about reading achievement scores in the United States over the past twenty-five years is not how they've declined, but just how *stable* they have been. Several researchers have reviewed and published detailed analyses of the state of reading in the United States, and nearly all of them have come to the same conclusion: Children in the United States are reading as well now as they did a generation ago, and maybe better (Berliner & Biddle, 1995; Bracey, 1997a).

The best evidence on reading achievement in the United States comes from a national system of examinations established back in the late 1960s by the federal government to determine how United States schoolchildren were performing in a variety of school subjects, especially reading and mathematics. These exams, collectively know as the National Assessment of Educational Progress, or the NAEP, are important barometers of educational achievement. Unlike commercial tests given by many school districts, such as the Comprehensive Test of Basic Skills or the Iowa Test of Basic Skills, the NAEP is given nationally to a representative sample of United States children, so that we can extrapolate more confidently from its results just how well the nation as a whole is doing.

Table 1.1 shows the reading scores of United States children at three age levels from the first year the NAEP was administered, 1971, to the most recent administration in 1996. The test is scored on a scale of 0 to 500. It is immediately apparent that, despite a few minor fluctuations, reading achievement has either stayed even or increased slightly over the past three decades. No decline whatsoever is indicated at any level.

Other indicators of reading achievement show similar stability or growth, including commercial tests at all levels, from the Iowa Test of Basic Skills to the Graduate Record Examination (see Berliner & Biddle, 1995, for details). Even very young children appear to be doing better than their age peers of two decades ago. Mayer (1997) reports that a 1992 national sample of five-to-seven-year-olds scored 5.1 points higher on the reading portion of the Peabody Individual Achievement Test (PIAT) than the same age children in 1970.[1]

Table 1.1

Average Reading Proficiency of 9-, 13-, and 17-Year-Olds
in the United States, 1971–1996

AGE	1971	1975	1980	1984	1988	1990	1992	1994	1996
9 years	208	210	215	211	212	209	211	211	212
13 years	255	256	259	257	258	257	260	258	259
17 years	285	286	286	289	290	290	290	288	287

Source: Campbell, Reese, O'Sullivan, and Dossey (1996), p. 106; Campbell, Voelkl, and Donahue (1997), p. 104.

Myth 2: Forty Percent of United States Children Can't Read at a Basic Level

There is no question that some children in the United States cannot read very well. But is it true, as some politicians and researchers have stated, that nearly *half* of our children are below a "basic" level in reading (McGuinness, 1997)? The claim has its origin in the way in which the United States Department of Education now has decided to report their biennial NAEP results, reports which themselves need some interpreting. During the early years of the NAEP tests, the Department released only the raw scores for each age level on its 0 to 500 scale, with no designations of what score was thought to constitute "basic" or "proficient" levels of reading. The designers of the NAEP test later decided, however, that simply reporting the raw scores was no longer adequate in order to judge the progress of United States schools. To give some supposed meaning to these scores, the Department decided it would determine how well students were reading by establishing what some have interpreted to be "objective" cutoff points, indicating the minimum score constituting "below basic," "basic," "proficient," and "advanced" reading for each age level tested.[2] The "basic" level for fourth-grade reading, for example, was fixed at a score of 208. In 1994, 40 percent of United States children scored below the "basic" cutoff of 208.

The problem with this approach lies in "objectively" determining where these cutoff points should be. Is it really possible to come up with a minimal level of competency in reading? One of the country's leading researchers and theorists in the area of educational statistics, Gene Glass, thinks not. Glass (1978), after reviewing the various methods proposed for creating "minimal" criterion scores of performance, concluded that all such efforts are necessarily arbitrary, amounting to little more than "pseudoquantification" (p. 239). One reason for such pessimism is not difficult to understand: One person's "below basic" is the next person's "proficient." It might be argued, though, that "experts" would certainly agree on what students should know at a given age, and indeed the NAEP levels were based on "collective judgements, gathered from a broadly representative panel of teachers, education specialists, and members of the general public" (Campbell, Donahue et al., 1996, p. 6). But what if Expert Panel A disagrees with Expert Panel B? And even if standards are agreed upon, the actual implementation of them will fall to a group of test writers, each of whom may write more or less difficult items. Glass noted that no amount of mathematical wizardry can make this problem of arbitrariness go away. Indeed, any teacher knows that you can make a test so easy that everyone passes or so difficult that everyone fails. Of course, such arbitrary cutoff points already exist in education and many other fields, but at least they are recognized as arbitrary, and not given the status of absolute or objective levels of competence.

The fallacy of obtaining "objective" definitions of "basic" reading abilities is illustrated by the real-world attempts to implement them. One may be tempted to think, for example, that while truly "objective" measures of competence are not possible, surely we can get those knowledgeable about reading to reach some common understanding about what a "basic" reading level looks like at a given grade level, right? One answer to this question is found in Table 1.2, which shows the percentage of students in 14 states who were judged to be "proficient" in reading at the third- and fourth-grade levels according to two different tests. In the first column is the

Table 1.2

Percentage of 3rd/4th Grade Students "Proficient" in Reading, 1994–95

STATE	% PROFICIENT ON NAEP EXAM (4TH GRADERS)	% PROFICIENT ON STATE EXAM (3RD/4TH GRADERS)	DIFFERENCE BETWEEN STATE AND NATIONAL ESTIMATES
Connecticut	38	48	10
Delaware	23	11	12
Georgia	26	67	41
Indiana	35	66	31
Kentucky	26	28	2
Louisiana	15	88	73
Maryland	26	34	8
New Hampshire	36	26	10
North Carolina	30	65	35
Rhode Island	32	65	33
South Carolina	20	82	62
Tennessee	27	62	35
Texas	26	79	53
Wisconsin	35	88	53

(from "Comparing Test Results," *Education Week,* January 15, 1997)

percentage as determined by the 1994 NAEP test; in the second column, the individual state's estimate based on its own choice of a standardized reading test. Note that most states established their cutoff scores based on the advice of their own expert panel, each no doubt as qualified as the next. Yet in almost every case states came up with different results—sometimes dramatically so—in the number of students who were thought to be good readers. Louisiana, for example, had 88 percent of its students reading at a proficient level on its own assessment, but only 15 percent on the NAEP test—a difference of 73 percentage points! Delaware judged only 11 percent of its students as reading proficiently but showed twice that (23 percent) as proficient on the NAEP tests. Wisconsin had only 35 percent of its children score at the proficient level on the NAEP, but judged an impressive 88 percent proficient on its own exam. Each exam, each panel, each state came up with a different determination of a "proficient" reader. Overall, there was an average difference of nearly 33 percentage points between the two estimates of proficient readers.

All "minimal," "basic," or "proficient" cutoff points on educational tests are necessarily relative. Of course, as in any normal distribution of scores, some students will be at the top of the curve, some at the bottom, and most right around average. The only thing we can really determine from reading tests (or math tests or social studies tests) is whether children are doing better or worse than their age peers of previous years. And what we know about such performance in reading is that it has been completely stable for the past two-and-a-half decades, as noted previously. If nearly half of children in the United States today are truly below a "basic" level of reading, then that has always been the case, which might make one wonder how the nation has managed to survive up to this point. An alternative interpretation, of course, is that the NAEP proficiency levels themselves are amiss.

Myth 3: Twenty Percent of Our Children Are Dyslexic

Closely related to the previous misconception that 40 percent of our students read below the "basic" level is another portentous-sounding figure that has been circulated widely in the media and in many academic circles; namely, that 20 percent of United States schoolchildren suffer from a "neurobehavioral disorder" known as "dyslexia," often referred to simply as a "reading disability" (Shaywitz et al., 1996). The research most often cited to support this claim is drawn from the results of the Connecticut Longitudinal Study (CLS), a large-scale project funded in part by the National Institute of Child Health and Human Development (Shaywitz, Escobar, Shaywitz, Fletcher, & Makuch, 1992; Shaywitz, Fletcher, Holahan, & Shaywitz, 1992; Shaywitz, Fletcher, & Shaywitz, 1994; Shaywitz, Shaywitz, Fletcher, & Escobar, 1990). The CLS tracked over 400 students from kindergarten through young adulthood, periodically measuring their Intelligence Quotient (IQ), reading achievement, and mathematical abilities, among other attributes. CLS researchers measured "reading disability" by two methods. The first is what is known as "discrepancy scores," which represent the difference between a child's actual reading achievement and what would be predicted based upon his IQ. The idea is that if you have a high IQ but are poor at reading, then something must be wrong with you. The actual size of the discrepancy used in the CLS

Table 1.3

Children Classified as Reading Disabled in the Connecticut
Longitudinal Study (N = 414)

	GRADE 1	GRADE 2	GRADE 3	GRADE 5
Number	25	32	31	24
Percentage	6.03%	7.76%	7.78%	5.79%

(from Shaywitz et al., 1990, p. 998; S. Shaywitz et al., 1992, p. 147)

studies was that recommended by the United States Department of Education, 1.5 standard deviations. This 1.5 standard deviations figure was thus their "cutoff" score used to determine who was reading "disabled" and who was not. Table 1.3 shows the number and percentage of children at four grade levels who were determined to have reading disabilities out of a total of 414 children.

In any given year, then, a little less than 8 percent fall into the category of reading disabled, using the 1.5 cutoff. Two important things need to be noticed about these results. First, and most importantly, the 1.5 standard deviations cutoff point is, like all such cutoff points for minimal competence, arbitrary. We could just as easily have used 1.25 or 1.75 or .5, each producing a different percentage of "neurobehaviorally" afflicted children—the sky's the limit. Second, even the 8 percent represented in Table 1.3 have not been shown in this research to be "dyslexic," if by "dyslexic" we mean a "*neurologically based* disorder in which there is unexpected failure to read," the definition used by the CLS team (S. Shaywitz et al., 1992, p. 145; emphasis added). This is because, quite simply, no neurological measures were administered to these particular children.[3] All that can be said from these findings is that around 8 percent of children in any given year will have a discrepancy of 1.5 standard deviations between their IQ and reading achievement, at least if they live in Connecticut.

The second approach used in classifying "dyslexic" children was to set the cutoff point for reading disabilities at the 25th percentile on a norm-referenced reading test, regardless of the child's IQ. In this case, the reading tests came from the Woodcock-Johnson Psycho-Educational Battery (W-J) (Woodcock & Johnson, 1977). Using the second-grade data (a total of 415 children), B. Shaywitz et al. (1992) found 63 children who scored below the 25th percentile cutoff (25 of whom also met the discrepancy criterion, the method described above), or a total of 15.18 percent. Seven others met the discrepancy criterion but not the percentile cutoff. Adding them to the total count, we get 70 out of 415, or 16.86 percent. Round it up, and you get 20 percent of United States children suffering from dyslexia.

It is necessary to recall how percentiles are arrived at in standardized tests in order to see that this second method of classifying "dyslexia" is no less arbitrary than the first. A standardized test like the W-J is typically given to a large sample of students who (ideally) are representative of the population as a whole that will use the test (in the case of the W-J, this "norming sample" of children came from 40 different communities tested back in the mid-70s [Woodcock & Johnson, 1977, pp. 28–29]). With a large enough representative sample, the scores will generally have something close to a "normal distribution," meaning that the spread of scores from low to high resembles the well-known bell curve. The majority of students will score somewhere in the middle, with progressively fewer at the top and bottom of the curve. The average or "mean" score in such a normally distributed, "unskewed" bell curve will be the point at which 50 percent of the students score above and 50 percent score below. Similar points along the distribution represent the scores below which a certain percentage of the sample population falls. The 25th percentile, for example, is the point below which 25 percent of the students scored. If you give this same test to another sample of students like the norming sample, you will find—*by definition*—that around 25 percent will score below the cutoff score for the 25th percentile.

Now, the CLS researchers found that, in their particular sample, only 15 percent of the students fell below the original W-J sample's 25th percentile score. The only conclusion that can be drawn from this result is that the children in the CLS sample were not comparable to the 1977 W-J sample and perhaps were somewhat better readers. But absolutely none of this adds up to the conclusion that 20 percent of United States children are dyslexic. That's because there is nothing significant about the 25th percentile cutoff point used in the CLS (or the 20th or the 30th or the 16th) in dividing those who do and do not have a "neurobehavioral" disorder, any more than the 1.5 discrepancy score used in the first method. Other researchers using a different criterion score would have come up with a different percentage. As in the case of the preceding myth, there is simply no objective way of arriving at such a determination from reading tests. The best we can say is that a certain percentage of students read below this arbitrary cutoff at this age. We can then choose to label (or mislabel) this group in a certain manner, but we have no reason to conclude, at least based on the CLS evidence, that they suffer from any neurological disorder or other biological defect.[4,5]

Myth 4: Children from the Baby Boomer Generation Read Better than Students Today

Some might object that signs of stability over the past two decades are misleading, that we must go back even farther than the 1960s and 1970s to observe large drops in reading achievement, perhaps to the 1950s or 1940s. McGuinness (1997), for example, argues that children who learned to read between 1955 and 1965 are better readers than those educated in more recent years. Her evidence comes from a study of adult literacy levels, the National Adult Literacy Survey (NALS), which was given by the United States Department of Education to a representative sample of United States adults in 1992 (Kirsch, Jungblut, Jenkins, & Kolstad, 1993). McGuinness notes that those between the ages of 35 and 44 at the time of the survey—and hence those who learned to read in the mid-1950s to mid-1960s—have higher reading scores than those of subsequent generations. This is proof, she claims, that schools are not as good as they once were.

What McGuinness is proposing here is problematic, to say the least: Can we really measure the effectiveness of schools 40 years ago by how well their graduates read today? What about the intervening 30 years of reading experience and education? We should hardly expect the reading proficiency of these adults to remain stagnant over time. Surely the reading scores of this same group of 35–44-year-olds from when they were still enrolled in school are better indicators of how well they performed as children than the NALS test, since fewer intervening variables exist to confound the results. We do, in fact, have reading achievement scores from a representative sample of children of this age cohort in the form of the high school NAEP scores from 1971 (for those who entered first grade in 1959 and were 38 at time of the NALS administration). As can be seen in Table 1.1, their scores are not much different (and slightly lower) than more recent graduates, indicating that baby boomers were not better readers as they exited schools than are today's graduates.

Moreover, an analysis by M. Cecil Smith (1995) of the same NALS data cited by McGuinness found that when we compare adults of *similar educational levels*—an important control, since higher levels of education lead to higher reading scores—those adults who reached majority age after 1987 (age 19–24 at the time of the survey) actually have slightly *higher* proficiency than older readers of similar educational experience who went through the school system back in the 1940s, 1950s, and 1960s. This superiority in reading achievement by young adults holds true on most of the literacy measures used in the study, even when a person's current reading habits are considered. In addition, 19- to 24-year-olds are just as likely to be avid readers as their older counterparts, whether we look at the reading of books, newspapers, or magazines.[6]

Additional evidence against McGuinness's claim comes from commercial tests that, while not given to a representative sample of United States students like the NAEP, are normed on a large group of schoolchildren and thus in some sense indicative of national performance. As Berliner and Biddle (1995) and Bracey (1997a) point out, the scores on these tests have been stable or rising since the 1950s.[7] The results of general intelligence tests, which date back to the early thirties, have also been climbing steadily since then (Berliner & Biddle, 1995), making any assertions about the superiority of a mythical "golden age" of education in the United States somewhat suspect.

Myth 5: Students in the United States Are Among the Worst Readers in the World

What will come as most surprising to many people is how the United States compares internationally in reading achievement: Our nine-year-olds ranked second in the world in the most recent round of testing conducted by the International Association for the Evaluation of Educational Achievement (IEA); our fourteen-year-olds ranked a very respectable 9th out of 31. United States schoolchildren are truly world-class in reading.[8] Table 1.4 reports the top ten countries at each age level tested, taken from Elley (1992).

It is important to note the range of scores at the two age levels. The United States came in second among nine-year-olds, with the next best-scoring country, Sweden, scoring 9 points lower and the fourth ranking nation, France, 16 points lower. Among the fourteen-year-olds, the United States ranked ninth out of 34, but

Table 1.4
Average Scores of 9-Year-Olds and 14-Year-Olds in Reading Achievement

9-YEAR-OLDS		14-YEAR-OLDS	
COUNTRY	MEAN SCORE	COUNTRY	MEAN SCORE
Finland	569	Finland	560
United States	547	France	549
Sweden	539	Sweden	546
France	531	New Zealand	545
Italy	529	Hungary	536
New Zealand	528	Iceland	536
Norway	524	Switzerland	536
Iceland	518	Hong Kong	535
Hong Kong	517	United States	535
Singapore	515	Singapore	534

(from Elley, 1992, Tables 3.1 & 4.1)

this is somewhat deceiving, since the United States was virtually tied with 5 other countries after fourth-place New Zealand.

Too Good to Be True?

A dissenting opinion on just how well United States schoolchildren perform over time and internationally is held by Walberg (1996), who argues that reading achievement has in fact declined since the early 1970s. Walberg compared the IEA scores from 1990–91 noted in Table 1.4 to the first IEA test given to 15 nations in 1970, with the scores from the two tests equated (Lietz, 1995, cited in Walberg). Walberg concluded that the scores did indeed decline, from 602 in 1970 to 541 in 1991 (using his adjusted scores).

Two problems exist with this analysis, however. First, it is not clear why the two IEA tests given 22 years apart should be preferred in measuring trends in United States reading performance over the United States Department of Education's own NAEP exam, which has not only been given more frequently (9 times since 1970), but was designed to be much more sensitive to a broader range of reading achievement (Binkley & Williams, 1996) than the IEA tests. Second, the IEA test has changed considerably since its first administration in 1970 (Elley, 1994). Unfortunately, the re-analysis of the scores upon which Walberg bases his comparisons is unpublished, making it difficult to know precisely how these "equated" scores were derived from what were markedly different tests. Elley, Schleicher, and Wagemaker (1994) note that common passages were used in the 1970 and 1991 assessments, but there is no indication in Walberg's report of whether the scores being compared were based upon these sections of the test.

Walberg also finds evidence for failing United States performance in a European study (Organization for Economic Cooperation and Development, 1995) in which scores of "reading efficiency" were computed for each country that participated in the IEA's 1990–91 test administration. This efficiency score comes from subtracting a country's average score for its nine-year-olds from that of its fourteen-year-olds, dividing by the age difference, and multiplying by five (for the five years difference) (OECD, 1995, p. 207). The result is said to indicate how much students "gained" or "lost" in the intervening period. Students in the United States, according to this measure, gained 124.9 points, less than the average gain of 159.6 points. From this Walberg concludes that United States schools don't do a very good job in reading achievement with students after the fourth grade or so.

But Bracey (1997b) notes that, by this same measure, the top-scoring country in the world, Finland, had the third worst "reading efficiency" among the countries compared, whereas the worst-scoring country in the OECD sample—Denmark—had the greatest efficiency, since its scores climbed the most between ages nine and fourteen. This should lead us to think that something may be amiss in the measure itself. In fact, Bracey points out that the relationship between a country's ranking on the OECD's efficiency scale for its nine-year-olds and its fourteen-year-olds was strongly negative (rank order correlation = −.69), suggesting that this rather odd measure of "progress" depends more on how poorly you start out rather than on true increases or declines in reading achievement.

Another critic, Andrew Coulson (1996) agrees that reading achievement has been mostly stable, but he still sees signs of decline among our high school seniors. He notes that comparable measures of adult literacy given in 1985 and 1992 (the Young Adult Literacy Survey and the National Adult Literacy Survey, respectively) to twenty-one- to twenty-five-year-olds showed "real" declines. A closer look at the data shows, in fact, rather small drops: Among whites, the decline was a mere 9 points on a 500 point scale, from 305 to 296. The largest drop was among Latinos, but the authors of the report note that there was a huge increase in the number of adults taking the test for whom English was not their first language, which would depress test scores regardless of how well schools were performing in reading instruction. Once again, there is little basis for arguing that reading performance has recently declined. Neither Walberg's nor Coulson's evidence, when examined more closely, show that students today are performing any worse than did previous generations.

Myth 6: The Number of Good Readers Has Been Declining, While the Number of Poor Readers Has Been Increasing

It is of course conceivable that, while the average performance of United States students has remained the same, the number of students "at the top" has been declining, and this indeed has been claimed by some critics (e.g., Murray & Herrnstein, 1992; Coulson, 1996). Considerable attention has been paid, for example, to the results of the Scholastic Aptitude Test (SAT), and slight declines in the numbers of stu-

Table 1.5
Percentage of Students Scoring at Highest Performance Levels
for Age on NAEP, 1971–1994

AGE	1971	1975	1980	1984	1988	1990	1992	1994
17-Year-Olds (Above 350)	7	6	5	6	5	7	7	7
13-Year-Olds (Above 300)	10	10	11	11	11	16	15	15
9-Year-Olds (Above 250)	17	16	19	18	19	20	17	18

(from Table 8.1, p. 130 in Campbell, Reese, et al., 1996)

dents scoring at the SAT's highest levels (Hirsch, 1996). While it is true that the number of students scoring above 700 on the SAT did decline, the numbers were never high (2.3 percent in 1966, 1.2 percent in 1995). More importantly, the large demographic changes in United States schools over the past three decades have almost certainly had an influence on these small drops in test scores. As Bracey (1997a) points out, the drops occurred primarily between 1966 and 1972, since which time the percentage of students scoring above 700 has remained stable. Claims of a general decline over many years are not warranted. Moreover, two studies that have attempted to control for the significant demographic shifts in the test pool since the early 1950s have found that the average declines during the 1960s and 1970s were rather small (see Bracey, 1997a).

But the most important point to keep in mind when discussing the SAT is that it is not a representative sample of United States high school students; it is not even a representative sample of college-bound seniors. It is a voluntary test that a large proportion of students take in some states (e.g., Connecticut, New York) and hardly any students take in other states (e.g., Iowa, North Dakota).[9] The NAEP tests, by contrast, are representative, and they indicate *no* decline in the percentage of students scoring at the highest levels, as Table 1.5 illustrates.

The performance levels given in Table 1.5 are generally the highest for which a given age group has scored since the NAEP tests began.[10] As can be seen, little change has occurred in the percentage of high-scoring students at any grade level, with the percentage of thirteen-year-olds scoring at the top levels showing an increase over the past three decades.

The flip side of the supposed decline of the "best and brightest" is that the number of poor readers has been increasing. Once again, the results from the nationally representative samples on the NAEP test show this not to be the case, as indicated in Table 1.6. The number of poor readers has remained fairly stable among all age groups (using the lowest cutoff points given by the NAEP reports).

Table 1.6
Percentage of Students Below Lowest Performance Levels by Age
on NAEP, 1971–1994

AGE	1971	1975	1980	1984	1988	1990	1992	1994
17-Year-Olds (Below 200)	4	4	3	2	1	2	3	3
13-Year-Olds (Below 200)	7	7	5	6	5	6	7	8
9-Year-Olds (Below 150)	9	7	5	8	7	10	8	8

(from Table 8.1, p. 130 in Campbell, Reese, et al., 1996). Scale is 0 to 500.

Myth 7: California's Test Scores Declined Dramatically Due to Whole Language Instruction

Some critics have not been satisfied with merely finding a crisis (or illness) where none exists. It has also become necessary to produce a guilty party to blame for our greatly exaggerated woes (Levine, 1996; Stewart, 1996). In this case, the villain is an approach to the teaching of reading called "whole language." The focus of these attacks have centered primarily on California, a state that at least nominally adopted a more "holistic" view of teaching language arts back in 1987 that, it is claimed, led to a steep decline in reading scores. California has become a national test case in reading instruction, and since many of the skills-oriented solutions to our current reading "crisis" are in large part a reaction to what happened there, it is worth examining the situation in some detail.

Two points are at issue in the case of California and its reading crisis. First, did California's reading test scores really "plummet" (Stewart, 1996, p. 23) to record lows after 1987? Second, was this sharp decline attributable to the adoption of a reading curriculum in the state in 1987 (CRTFR, 1995) that emphasized reading books and decreasing (but not eliminating) phonics and skills instruction? It turns out that the answer to both of those questions is "no."

California Dreamin': The Surf Was Never Up

The popular wisdom about California's decline stemmed mostly from the release of two sets of test scores: the 1992 and 1994 NAEP scores, and results of the state's own California Learning Assessment System (CLAS). In both the 1992 and 1994 state NAEP rankings, California fared rather poorly: Of the 41 participating states and territories in 1992, California ranked 38th; in 1994, it was tied for last (Campbell, Donahue, Reese, & Phillips, 1996). Rank scores are, of course, slightly misleading, since a difference of a few points can cause a state to rise or drop in rank if the states are clustered closely together. But even when this clustering is taken into account, California still did not fare well: In 1992, the state was in the bottom third, and in 1994, in the bottom quarter (Campbell, Donahue et al., 1996). Clearly, California was performing relatively poorly compared to the rest of the nation.

But performing poorly is not the same as getting *worse*. To show a decline, one must look at scores from both the beginning and the end of the time period in question. Herein lies the problem: State-level NAEP scores are unavailable before 1992, and the tests are not equivalent to any other standardized reading measure. As such, the NAEP data cannot tell us anything about whether scores went up or down after the implementation of the literature-based curriculum.

The second set of data cited to show California's supposed drop, the California Learning Assessment System (CLAS), suffers from the same lack of comparability. The CLAS tests were administered only twice, in the 1992–93 and 1993–94 school years. Like the NAEP scores, they are not comparable to previous test scores and tell us nothing about how California students read before and after the 1987 Framework adoption. (In fact, the two years are not even comparable to each other, due to changes made in the test after the first year of its administration.) Ironically, the 1993–94 results indicated that more than three-fourths of California's students could read at a "basic" level (McQuillan, 1996, in press: d).

The only test score data available both before and after the implementation of the "holistic" 1987 Language Arts Framework are the California Achievement Program scores. As can be seen in Table 1.7, there is no indication of dramatic drops or increases. Some scores went up, some went down, but for the most part things were remarkably stable. California's third graders, for example, were performing at the same level in 1990 as they were in 1985, which would be unlikely if the 1987 Framework resulted in a dramatic decline in test scores.[11]

Despite repeated claims to the contrary, then, there is no evidence that California reading scores have declined markedly over the past ten years, and sufficient data to suggest that there has been little change in achievement since the 1987 Framework adoption. This stability of test scores is remarkable in light of the declining financial status of the California's schools, a decline that has been largely ignored in

Table 1.7
California Achievement Program Raw Scores for 3rd, 6th, 8th, and 12th Grades, 1984–1990

GRADE	1984	1985	1986	1987	1988	1989	1990
3rd	268	274	280	282	282	277	275
6th	249	253	260	260	265	262	261
8th	250	240	243	247	252	256	257
12th	236	241	240	246	250	248	251

(from Guthrie et al., 1988, 1993)

the debates over reading achievement in the state. Indeed, the teachers of California are to be commended for managing to keep scores from plunging given the limited resources they have been allotted (see Chapter 7).

Whole Language to Blame?

The second part of the argument used to promote a renewed emphasis on skills instruction was that whole language was the cause of California's (nonexistent) decline and (very real) low national ranking. As noted earlier, it is true that California ranked relatively low among the states. Is a literature-based curriculum or whole language to blame? Another look at the 1992 NAEP data reveals that the answer appears to be "no." As part of the assessment, fourth-grade teachers were asked to indicate their methodological approach to reading as "whole language," "literature-based," and/or "phonics." The average scores for each type of approach were then compared, and those children in classrooms with heavy emphasis on phonics clearly did the worst. Children in whole language-emphasis classrooms (reported by 40 percent of the teachers) had an average score of 220, those in literature-based classrooms had a score of 221 (reported by 49 percent of the teachers), and students in phonics classrooms (reported by 11 percent of the teachers) came in last with an average score of 208 (NCES, 1994, p. 284). Similar patterns were observed in the 1994 NAEP results (Campbell, Donahue et al., 1996). If these data on teacher-self-report are accurate, and reading method is a primary determinant of reading scores in a state, there is little reason to blame whole language for California's reading woes.[12]

*   *   *

Many things are wrong with United States schools, and, as I stated at the beginning of this chapter, I have no interest in ignoring legitimate problems we face in the area of literacy development. But false crises and distorted views of student achievement can only distract us from the real concerns of parents, teachers, and policymakers. Instead, we need to have some understanding of what reading is and know some of the most important factors influencing reading achievement. In the following chapters, I examine some basic theories of language and literacy acquisition, a few competing explanations of the critical variables related to reading achievement, and what I believe to be the real barriers to improving literacy in our low-achieving schools.

2

Getting Started:
What Do You Need to Learn
How to Read?

The subject of how children learn how to read has attracted an extraordinary amount of attention, both from the popular media and in the scientific literature. Indeed, the intense focus on early reading has taken on the overtones of an all-out war in which opposing sides are thought to do battle. The purpose of this chapter is to attempt to lay out a general framework for understanding how children learn to read, setting out in an admittedly simple but, I hope, comprehensible manner some of the principal factors that need to be taken into account in explaining why some children succeed where others fail. Once that is done, it will be easier to understand where the true controversies lie in the debates over reading, and which evidence is appropriate in judging competing prescriptions about what schools should do to help struggling readers.

A General Model of Language Acquisition

Stephen Krashen (1981, 1996b) has proposed that we acquire languages when we engage in a single, all-important act: when we understand messages. More precisely, Krashen states that acquisition results from the comprehension of messages that contain elements of language slightly above our current level of competence. This general relationship has been supported by evidence in both first (L1) and second (L2) language acquisition for both oral (Asher, 1994; Cross, 1977; Hart & Risley, 1995; Krashen, 1981, 1985; Swaffer & Woodruff, 1978) as well as written language (Anderson, Wilson, & Fielding, 1988; Elley & Mangubhai, 1983; Elley, 1991; Krashen, 1993; Taylor, Frye, & Maruyama, 1990).[1]

Figure 2.1 is a representation of this general model of language acquisition, where the act of comprehending messages results in language acquisition. The notion that we acquire language by understanding messages is also central to Ken and Yetta Goodman's (Goodman, 1967; Goodman & Goodman, 1979) and Frank Smith's (1973, 1994) theories of literacy acquisition. I will refer to this idea that reading

15

Figure 2.1
A General Model of Language Acquisition

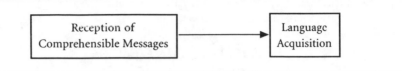

development is a result of understanding meaningful written language as the Goodman-Smith Model, since these researchers have been the most instrumental in providing the intellectual and empirical basis for it.[2]

How Do We Understand Messages?

It is useful to consider just what takes place when we try to make sense of language, specifically written language, since our focus here is on reading. As it turns out, reading involves using both the information that is present on the written page, as well as the information we already have in our minds. Smith (1994) notes that reading is, like all comprehension, relating the known to the unknown. We do not begin our encounter with written language (sometimes called simply *print* or *text*) with a *tabula rasa,* or blank slate; we are able to reduce the uncertainty of what is on the page by what we already know. As an experienced reader picking up a book in English, for example, you know where to look for the beginning, which side is up, where the page numbers are likely to be located, and so forth, based on your previous experiences with text. Similarly, when you look at words on a page, you know that only so many likely alternatives exist for the way letters combine to make words, words combine to make sentences, and, on a larger scale, sentences combine to convey the particular meaning of a text. Of course, we are sometimes wrong, sometimes surprised, and on occasion we read more slowly or reread to understand the (unlikely) alternatives we encounter. It takes longer to choose among more alternatives, so that the more unlikely the concept or word or even letter, the more time we need to decide which option "fits" or makes sense. This highlights the fact that comprehension is a normal activity where complete uncertainty is relatively rare; reading is something we expect to make sense.

The information we use to reduce uncertainty—what Smith refers to interchangeably as "nonvisual" information, background knowledge, or "context"—includes all we know about language: how markings on the page form letters and words, the meaning of words, how sentences go together, the topic of what is read, the sounds letters make, and many other things. Some of this background knowledge will be more useful than others, and some (such as the sounds letter make) may only be used as a last resort, when all other ways of making sense have broken down.

Ironically, as Smith (1994) points out, we use the actual visual information, the markings on the page, as little as possible to make sense of what we read. To attempt to focus on each letter or each word would overload our capacity to process information, like the slow reader who, by the time he or she has reached the end of a sentence, has forgotten the first word. Luckily, our background information is so powerful and able to reduce uncertainties at every level of reading—word, sentence, and beyond—that fluent reading can take place despite the enormous amount of visual information present in the text.

Reading is making sense of text, then, at the highest level possible: We "read" not individual letters or even words, but *meaning* as our eyes scan the page. When we come across an alternative that surprises or confuses us, we slow down and, perhaps, focus on a smaller group of words. If that doesn't help, we may look at each word to try to understand what is taking place. If the word itself is not familiar to us, we may resort to other strategies to figure out its meaning, including trying to "recode" it into sound by groups of letters or even, as a final resort, by individual letters. Notice, however, that this chain of events takes place only if comprehension breaks down, only if, as we are going along extracting meaning from the larger units of visual information (sentences, phrases), we run into trouble, confused by some unlikely alternatives to what we think should come next.

Beginning readers, of course, have less knowledge of how the printed page is constructed, and less nonvisual information to reduce the number of alternatives they often face when reading. When comprehension breaks down, they may more often resort to ways of attempting to get the meaning of a particular word, including the possibility of using the sounds of the word's letters. This does not mean, however, that sound is essential to reading, or that fluent reading necessarily involves such a letter-by-letter, sound-by-sound "decoding." The use of sound in reading is one strategy for trying to make sense of the written text, but by no means the only or primary one.

Access, Assistance, and Acquisition

Knowing how we go about comprehending written language does not give us a very complete picture, however, of why some people read well and others not so well or not at all. To help answer these questions we need to expand our model outlined above by integrating into it two additional factors: the access we have to written language "input" (that is, reading materials) and the types of external assistance we may receive in helping us understand these written messages. Variations in the amount of reading materials available for us to comprehend will in part determine over time how much we read, and as a consequence, how well we read. Likewise, the types of outside help we get in understanding written messages from sources aside from the text itself—such as from teachers, parents, and the like—may facilitate (or hinder) how well we can make sense of what we read.

Access

What is often ignored in discussions of language and literacy acquisition, but logically implied in our Expanded Model of reading acquisition (refer to Figure 2.2 on page 20), is a *source* of written language input, or more simply, reading materials. We know from studies of second-language (L2) acquirers, for example, that access to language input as measured by how long a person lives in a country is positively related to the person's level of language acquisition, assuming that the messages encountered are comprehensible (i.e., the person is at least at an intermediate level of proficiency) and that the person has interaction with their surroundings (Krashen, 1976). Similarly, evidence exists that access to written input—reading materials—is also associated with more literacy development (Elley, 1992; Krashen, 1985, 1989, 1995). Although clearly one must actually "receive" the input by listening or reading in order to acquire language, large variations in the supply of input indirectly affect the level of language acquisition, and may explain large individual differences in proficiency.[3] One of the central tenets of this book is to argue that access to reading materials (written language input) is perhaps as important if not more so than other explanations of reading difficulties.

Two Types of Assistance

Once we have access to written language, how are we able to understand it? As noted above, our previous experiences with text will give us a great deal of useful knowledge in making sense of print. But we can also receive assistance from other, more capable readers, especially during our initial attempts at reading. This outside help given to us as children learning how to read is often simply called "instruction," but in order to understand more precisely how this assistance plays a role in reading, it is useful to classify it into two types: "metalinguistic" assistance and "elaborative" assistance. The claim here is that both types of "instruction" or assistance may be helpful in comprehending written language, even though neither is, strictly speaking, required.

Metalinguistic Assistance

The term *metalinguistic* means literally "beyond language," and is used here to mean knowledge about the way in which the language system itself works, a knowledge that we have explicitly and consciously (in Krashen terms, "learning" [1981]). Metalinguistic assistance is thus the help we get from more capable readers about how written language is put together. This includes things such as being provided information about how sounds and letters correspond, doing exercises aimed at improving one's awareness of how speech can be broken down into smaller units of sound, and being taught rules of grammar. Such explicit knowledge may be useful to us at times in understanding written input, especially when our background knowledge and the context of the printed page are insufficient to help us make sense of the message being conveyed.

Smith (1994) gives a good example of how one type of conscious, metalinguistic knowledge can be of help in comprehending text. Suppose a child is confronted with the following sentence but is unable to read the last word:

The man came riding in on his *horse.*

Knowledge that the *h* at a beginning of a word makes a certain sound would reduce the number of possibilities that the reader had to choose from. She would know, for example, the word could not be *car* or *train*. Explicitly teaching a child the sounds that letters make could contribute somewhat to comprehension of text and thus indirectly to reading acquisition.

Giving metalinguistic assistance is what I will refer to as "*formal* instruction." For beginning literacy, this typically takes place in formal settings like school when children are taught the alphabet and how sounds and letters go together ("phonics"), although parents sometimes also give their children limited metalinguistic knowledge at home by teaching them letter shapes and sounds (Durkin, 1966; Yaden, Smolkin, & Conlon, 1989). Note, however, that one can possess metalinguistic knowledge without being taught it—such knowledge may, that is, be discovered on one's own. Moustafa (1995, 1997) points out that children may come to understand how sounds and letters correspond through inductive use of analogy, comparing the parts of known words with unknown words. For example, a child who can read *green* and *back* can figure out how to pronounce nonsense words like *grack* by this very strategy.

One of the long-standing controversies in reading instruction is just how much, if any, formal, metalinguistic instruction children need to learn how to read. Some have claimed that it is absolutely essential in reading acquisition (e.g., Share, 1995), and that the presence or lack of such instruction can explain why some children ultimately succeed or fail in reading. Others have taken the position advocated here, that metalinguistic assistance is but one type of help ("instruction") children can receive, helpful to some limited extent for some children when desired or requested, usually in the context of trying to make sense of text.

Elaborative Assistance

By "elaborative assistance" I mean all other types of help given readers to make sense of language other than that related to how the language system itself is constructed; that is, information other than metalinguistic instruction. In the case of a child acquiring her first language, elaborative assistance may consist of things such as "semantic contingency" (continuing on about the topic introduced by the child's previous statement), a slower rate of speech, restatement of the message, using "here-and-now" topics, and similar devices (Newport, Gleitman, & Gleitman, 1977; Snow, 1983). All of these actions or strategies help children understand the messages being directed at them by giving them additional clues as to the meaning of the input they are exposed to. Similarly, second-language teachers use elaborative methods such as rephrasing or restating their messages, slowing their rates of speech, using props or gestures to give clues to their meaning, all in an attempt to make the language more comprehensible (Freed, 1980; Krashen, 1981). The focus is not on the structure of language system *per se*, but on understanding the meaning of the message.

In the acquisition of written language, elaborative assistance may be provided through verbal explanations of the story, giving the child an oral explanation of the background or the meaning of words. It may include reference to illustrations of the text, and how they help convey the message of the printed page. Studies of storybook reading, for example, show that parents give precisely this type of elaborative assistance about the story by describing the pictures, explaining the meaning of words, and giving background information on topics that appear in the story (Snow & Ninio, 1986; Smolkin, Conlon, & Yaden, 1988; Yaden, 1988). The focus of elaborative assistance is on making the meaning of the written language comprehensible, rather than consciously describing the language system itself.

Reformulation of the Model

Figure 2.2 restates our hypothesis for reading acquisition with the clarifications noted above, adapting that proposed by Krashen (1993). The model predicts that an increase in access to reading materials will tend to lead to an increase in the amount of reading, which in turn leads to higher levels of reading acquisition. This reception can be facilitated by both elaborative and metalinguistic external assistance, although neither is necessary.[4]

Counter Arguments on Reading

Several researchers have advocated positions contrary to the model outlined above. It has been claimed, for instance, that metalinguistic assistance plays not just a helpful role in learning how to read, but a critical one, and that certain forms of explicit instruction must be provided to nearly all children. As a consequence, some often expensive and sweeping pedagogical proposals to improve reading achievement have been proposed that include, among other things, a strong emphasis on "training" children in certain metalinguistic "skills" that are thought essential to reading. Understanding the factors that influence reading acquisition is thus important not merely from a theoretical perspective, but from a practical one as well. The reason is simple: The resources available to schools to improve literacy achievement are limited. Money devoted to programs to provide, for example, more intensive skills instruction is money that will *not* be available for other things, such as books or libraries or helping teachers. It is therefore necessary to discuss the objections and opposing arguments to the Goodman-Smith view of reading, objections that we will group under four major headings (Stanovich, 1993):

1. *The Role of Phonology and Metalinguistic Instruction in Reading:* It is claimed that explicit, metalinguistic instruction is essential for the children to learn how to read, and by extension that lack of such instruction can explain variations in

Figure 2.2
Expanded Model of Reading Acquisition

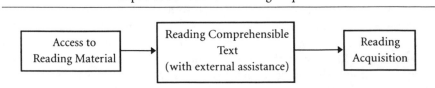

reading achievement. This instruction must include (at minimum) training in how sounds correspond to letters, and how speech can be broken down into smaller units of sound ("phonemic awareness").

2. *The Use of Context:* It is claimed that good readers actually make less use of "context" than poor ones while reading. This finding is said to disprove the Goodman-Smith view that reading is a process involving the use of background knowledge to reduce the number of unlikely alternatives in making sense of text.

3. *Eye Movement Research:* Recent studies on the manner in which the eyes fixate on words in a text are thought to show that context does not facilitate reading, again contrary to what Goodman and Smith are said to have proposed.

4. *Method Comparisons:* Studies comparing methods of teaching reading that emphasize metalinguistic assistance such as training students on sound-letter correspondences ("phonics") are said to produce superior results to "meaning-emphasis" teaching methods such as "whole language." This indicates that resources are best spent focusing instruction on such metalinguistic training to improve reading proficiency.

The next three chapters are devoted to addressing the rather complex set of issues raised in the first objection, that sound and metalinguistic awareness are crucial to reading acquisition and fluent reading. Chapter 3 will review studies on the necessity of metalinguistic assistance in order to learn how to read. Chapter 4 will discuss more indirect but still very suggestive evidence on the types of assistance readers benefit from by examining cases of "early" readers. Chapter 5 focuses on the claims made concerning phonological awareness and reading. The last three objections are all covered in Chapter 6, which will discuss research on context, eye movements, and method comparison studies. Finally, in Chapter 7, I argue that efforts to improve reading achievement need first to be focused on issues of access to reading materials, without which no instructional program can succeed.

3

What Does It Take
to Get the Alphabetic Principle?

One of the central theoretical and practical issues in reading acquisition is the role of formal instruction as we've defined it here: explicit, metalinguistic assistance. Is it possible, for example, that children can learn to read without such instruction? Is consciously learning about the written language system absolutely essential for all children learning how to read, or is its contribution more modest, one of being perhaps helpful to some children but not the key variable in initial reading acquisition? Our position stated in the previous chapter is that while some children *can* be assisted by a small amount of explicit teaching under certain circumstances, they benefit primarily from being exposed to print in a meaningful environment with appropriate forms of elaborative assistance.

Central to the dispute over what role metalinguistic instruction has in reading acquisition (and subsequently the amount of resources that should be devoted to it) is the proposition that, at least in English, children must first grasp the "alphabetic principle" in learning how to read. The alphabetic principle has been defined by Share (1995) as knowledge of both how sounds connect to letters (sound-letter correspondence) and "phonemic awareness," the conscious knowledge that speech can be segmented or divided somewhat artificially into minimal units of sound ("phonemes"). Phonemic awareness is the ability to divide, say, the word "cat" into three separate phonemes, "cuh," "ah," and "tuh," or in proper linguistics notation, /k/, /a/, and /t/. A grasp of the alphabetic principle is thought to give us the ability to "recode" or "sound out" written words, converting letters into sounds.

Two claims, then, have been made concerning this relationship: (1) the alphabetic principle (sound-letter correspondence and phonemic awareness) is necessary for a child to learn how to read; and (2) children must typically be taught the two above-mentioned components explicitly (Adams, 1990; Ehri & Wilce, 1985; Share, 1995; Stanovich, 1993). Share, for example, has stated that preliterate children who are exposed to print have "not been found to spontaneously induce discovery of the alphabetic principle," and that therefore "explicit instruction" is necessary to "bring

22

the decoding possibilities of an alphabetic orthography to a child's attention" (1995, p. 160).

The first claim has been disputed by a number of other researchers. Smith (1973, 1994) and Goodman (1996), for example, have argued that the ability to recode words into sound is not a prerequisite to reading, although it remains one resource at a child's disposal in her attempts to make sense of text. (We will discuss the role of phonology in reading more thoroughly in Chapter 5.)[1] This chapter will focus instead on the claim that children *must* be explicitly taught the alphabetic principle in order to acquire it. I will argue first that the studies cited by Share (1995) and others, while consistent with a strong version of what we may call the "Instruction Hypothesis," are insufficient to support the claim that explicit instruction is necessary (rather than merely helpful); and second, that it is equally plausible that the alphabetic principle, and more importantly, the ability to read, come primarily from exposure to comprehensible text with appropriate elaborative assistance, even without any significant amount of explicit, metalinguistic instruction.

Two Views on the Naturalness of Reading

Goodman and Goodman (1979) have posited that the acquisition of reading shares fundamental similarities with oral language acquisition: "Children learn to read and write in the same way and for the same reason that they learn to speak and listen. That way is to encounter language in use as a vehicle for communicating meaning" (p. 138). Drawing upon Halliday's (1969) categorization of the functions of oral language, Goodman and Goodman state that written language is acquired for similar uses and along a similar developmental path. The focus of both the beginning and proficient reader, Goodman and Goodman contend, is always on meaning, and a "high level of conscious awareness of the [linguistic] units and system" is not necessary to their task. Such metalinguistic knowledge of text (e.g., letter-sound correspondences) is acquired largely as a *consequence* of that concentration on meaning. In other words, explicit metalinguistic knowledge is not needed before one begins reading, but is largely developed while reading. Smith (1983) makes a similar point by stating that learning about the particular properties of written language comes most often from "hearing written language read aloud" (p. 47) and not primarily from a program of metalinguistic instruction.

Several theorists have criticized this position and have instead proposed that initial reading acquisition consists of movement through a series of stages that at some point requires explicit, metalinguistic assistance. Gough and Hillinger's (1980) two-stage model is probably the most straightforward of these proposals and illustrates the basic principle of the others (Ehri, 1992; cf. Stuart & Coltheart, 1986). Their first stage is "logographic" or "paired associate" learning of words, where children use distinct visual features of the word itself or the context associated with text as "cues" to remember the word. Hence the child might focus on the "hook" of the *J* in *John* to identify this word, or the double, stacked circles of the letter *B* to remember *Bob*. Gough and Hillinger argue, however, that this first-stage strategy is limited and unproductive; eventually the child runs out of distinctive features with which to "memorize" in this fashion. They hold instead that readers must at some junction make reference to the sound a word would make in order to store it in memory, since "it defies the imagination to suppose that the child could learn 50,000 items [an adult's reading vocabulary] by arbitrary associations" (p. 186).[2]

The second stage is "cryptoanalysis," or what others have called "alphabetic" reading (Ehri, 1992). Here children learn that letters or groups of letters represent sounds, and that this correspondence allows one to "recode" written words into sound, which (if in the child's oral vocabulary) he can then identify. In other words, this stage is marked by the acquisition of the alphabetic principle. Ehri (1992) breaks this stage up into three intermediate stages (partial, full, and consolidated alphabetic), but the end result is the same: Children are able to link letters or groups of letters to the pronunciation of words. Eventually, children are able to identify most words automatically without this constant recoding because "the brain processes the word's pronunciation and meaning without any effort directed at decoding the word" (Gaskins, Ehri, Cress, O'Hara, & Donnelly, 1996, p. 317). Gough and Hillinger argue that the movement from logographic to alphabetic word identification cannot be accomplished by children on their own—it is a qualitative "jump" that requires explicit, metalinguistic assistance.

Share (1995) advances a slightly different view of how children learn to read, which he terms an "item-based" rather than "stage-based" acquisition of recoding ability. Rather than posit a primarily logographic stage followed by an alphabetic one, Share holds that children use phonological information to identify words at various stages depending on their frequency and familiarity, and that only less familiar words that appear relatively infrequently ("low-frequency words") require recoding. Even so, the initial ability to recode must normally be taught, according to Share, so in practice his position is similar to Ehri's and Gough's.

Problematic Evidence on the Acquisition of the Alphabetic Principle

Two types of studies have been cited to support the position that formal, metalinguistic instruction is necessary for acquiring the alphabetic principle. The first type are examinations of the effects of "environmental print" exposure; that is, written language that commonly appears in the environment of children usually associated with some symbol or logo, such as "McDonald's" along side a pair of golden arches. The second type of evidence are "training" studies of children who are not yet able to read independently, where they are exposed to text and then tested on their ability to perform tasks related to sound-letter correspondence or "decoding." Each type of evidence suffers from its own particular shortcomings that make the available data ambiguous at best. The environmental print studies fail to take into account the types of contextual support available to children in their encounters with print. The training studies underestimate the duration and amount of input that may be needed for acquisition to take place. Let us take a look at examples of each type of evidence.

Environmental Print Studies:
The Problems of Overspecification

The distinction between metalinguistic and elaborative assistance noted in Chapter 2 dealt with help given by another, more proficient reader, such as a parent, teacher, or older sibling. Clearly this is not the only, or even most common, type of "elaborative" help available to children learning to read. Text is often found in environments that contain what is referred to as "extralinguistic" information, or information in addition to the language itself. This includes pictures, illustrations, logos, or symbols that give clues to the meaning of the text and render assistance from a more capable reader unnecessary. As Krashen has pointed out (personal communication), these clues can sometimes provide so much information that reference to the actual text is unnecessary for comprehension. The result is text that is *overspecified*. An illustrated book where the entire story can be understood perfectly makes the text redundant and is an example of an overspecified text. Conversely, the text could have too few extralinguistic clues for a beginning reader to comprehend the message, making it *underspecified*. The ideal situation is when elaborative clues are somewhere between these two extremes. When text is properly specified, the background information the reader brings to bear in comprehending the text helps her reduce the number of possible alternatives in meaning, but *does not eliminate them*. Some attention to the text itself must occur to understand the message.[3]

Acquisition under properly specified conditions may be incremental in nature, similar to that described by Nagy, Herman, and Anderson (1985) in their examination of vocabulary acquisition. Nagy and his colleagues found that unknown words can be acquired gradually by a reader through several exposures to them in meaningful contexts, with the reader picking up a bit more of the meaning with each pass. Under such conditions, exposure to text may lead to incremental increases too small to be detected by all-or-nothing measures such as simple pass/fail tests (i.e., know / don't know the word).

Discussions of whether being exposed to meaningful print alone can lead to certain aspects of reading acquisition must take these distinctions into account. We would not expect, for example, that children exposed to "environmental print" that contained text embedded in a lot of extralinguistic clues to necessarily acquire any insights into the linguistic elements of the text, since the context surrounding the print in effect replaces the text in conveying the meaning. For example, seeing the golden arches helps a child identify McDonald's without any attention paid to the actual name.

This prediction is confirmed by the available research. Masonheimer, Drum, and Ehri (1984) studied one hundred three- to five-year-old children who could identify at least eight popular "environmental print" signs (e.g., Pepsi, Carl's Jr.). The children were tested to see whether they could read those same words without the contextual support provided by the pictures or graphic information that normally accompanies them (e.g., no golden arches with the word *McDonald's*). In addition, these environmental print "experts" were also given tests to see whether they could recognize some common words drawn from beginning or "primer" reading materials printed in isolation on index cards. Of the one hundred children, only six of the children were able to read any of the primer words or read more than one of the eight environmental print words without the accompanying contextual support. The researchers conclude that reading words does not "evolve directly out of environmental print experiences" (p. 265). A partial replication of Masonheimer et al. by Stahl and Murray (1993) yielded essentially the same results.

As stated earlier, this interpretation is correct: Children do not need to attend to the text when the extralinguistic clues convey all of the required meaning. Exposure to this type of print is *not* sufficient to lead to the ability to read "bare" text in and of itself, *nor has that been claimed* (Goodman, 1986; Harste, Burke, & Woodward, 1982). Children may need exposure to other types of text—properly specified—for the alphabetic principle to be acquired.[4] Exposure to environmental print may lead, however, to incremental increases in other types of print knowledge, as we shall see below. In any case, environmental print studies cannot be considered supporting evidence that metalinguistic instruction is critical to reading acquisition.

Short Exposures and Impoverished Input

Some variation exists among children in terms of the rate of acquisition of various linguistic elements in oral language, even though they appear to follow a general developmental path (Brown, 1973) over an extended period of time. Similarly, we should expect that acquisition of the aspects of written language will take place at varying rates over a long period, and may require considerable amount of exposure to input. It appears untenable to posit, for example, that an infant exposed only to a few hours of a language containing a given grammatical structure would extract all of the necessary linguistic information contained in the input to acquire that structure. Such a test is equally inappropriate in written language acquisition. Yet the claim that explicit metalinguistic instruction is essential for learning how to read is based in part on studies that provide such limited input. The following three studies are among those cited by Share (1995) and illustrate the methodological flaws of this sort of evidence:

> *Byrne (1992):* Byrne conducted a series of studies to show that children need to be taught that speech can be broken down into smaller units—phonemes—and how these phonemes correspond to letters. In one experiment, for example, a group of eleven children were taught the words *bat* and *fat* in isolation. Most children were able to identify the two words after about ten minutes. This training constituted the entire "exposure to print" for the experiment. The subjects were then given several new words representing minimal pairs, distinguished only by their first letters, either *b* or *f* (e.g., *bell* and *fell*, *big* and *fig*). On average, children could not distinguish the new words above the level of chance, although individual scores were not provided.
>
> The amount of print the children were exposed to—two words—and the ten minute duration make Byrne's conclusions very questionable. Byrne himself acknowledged that two items may not be enough for children to acquire the req-

uisite phonemic representation. In a subsequent experiment, he increased the amount of words shown to the children—to four, still clearly not sufficient to test any hypothesis on the effects of print exposure.

Seymour and Elder (1986): Seymour and Elder's study is cited by Share (1995) and others as demonstrating that even long-term exposure to text does not lead children to gaining insights into the alphabetic principle. The researchers looked at twenty-six children (ages 4.5 to 5.5) in a first grade classroom over a year's time. The children were taught to read by the "Look-Say" method plus some "phonics-based" instruction in spelling. The teacher used a "whole-word" method, where words were "taught [120 words] by presentation on flash cards and in illustrated booklets for practice in identification and naming" over the course of one school year (p. 6). The emphasis on memorizing individual words can be seen in the way the researchers, one of whom spent about two days per week in the classroom, discussed "reading" with the children: "Do you remember any [words] you learned this week?" and "Is this one of your reading words?" (p. 19). The test of the children's derivation of letter-sound correspondence was a series of isolated word lists given throughout the year, on which appeared both taught and new words. Very few of the children were able to pronounce any of the novel words.

Despite a long period of exposure, Seymour and Elder provided the children in this study with very impoverished input. It appears that little connected, meaningful print was used in the instruction. Seymour and Elder demonstrated that focusing on individual word memorization via flash cards in a print-poor environment is not a good method of teaching reading.

Ehri and Sweet (1991): Ehri and Sweet examined which factors were associated with success in "fingerpoint-reading" by children. Thirty pre-readers who had received no formal instruction in reading nor had participated in storybook reading in school were given pretests in letter knowledge, isolated word recognition, and phonemic awareness, among other things. The treatment consisted of the experimenters reading a story to the child several times, pointing to the words as they did, followed by the child reading and pointing to the words. The storybook sessions took place over two days, with a total of forty to sixty minutes per child. Following the sessions, the child was asked to read isolated lines of text, isolated words in the text, and point to certain words in the text as the experimenter said them. Among the conclusions of the authors were that "even novice word readers [those who could recognize at least one preprimer word prior to the treatment] did not learn to read many individual words out of context as a result of fingerpointing-reading practice" (p. 454).

Even in this brief exposure, some gains were apparently made by the children. Ten of the subjects (28 percent) were able to tell the difference between the text they had read in the story and an altered text substituted in the same book, and five children (14 percent) who could not read any of the preprimer words on the pretest were able to read some of the words when presented with the complete text and exhibited the ability to segment blends into phonemes. This illustrates they may have acquired some knowledge of print/letters even from the short exposure, similar to the incremental acquisition noted earlier in the vocabulary acquisition studies by Nagy (e.g., Nagy, Herman, and Anderson, 1985).[5] Other studies discussed by Share (1995) suffer from similar flaws of very brief exposures to a limited amount of comprehensible text (Carnine, 1977; Byrne & Fielding-Barnsley, 1989; Ehri & Wilce, 1987a, 1987b; Scott & Ehri, 1990).

Acquisition of the Alphabetic Principle Without Metalinguistic Instruction: Suggestive Evidence on Elaborative Assistance

The evidence put forth by Share and others to support the necessity of consciously teaching children about the metalinguistic properties of written language in early reading acquisition is insufficient or at best ambiguous. Other studies, while not without faults, suggest instead that the critical element in learning how to read, including the acquisition of the alphabetic principle, is exposure to comprehensible text. Reading acquisition appears to take place as long as text is provided in appropriate, comprehensible contexts, and is of sufficient quantity and duration.

There are several studies of how children first come to make sense of written language, done by researchers in the beginning or "emergent" literacy field. These investigations have examined the effects of exposure to print over a long period of time among young children, usually before they begin attending school, and typically with more varied types of input than those used in the experimental training studies discussed above. While it is not, in most cases, possible to determine whether the children in these studies have received systematic, formal metalinguistic instruction, in most instances it seems unlikely, or at the very least, that the metalinguistic assistance given was rather limited. Research on early readers (Durkin, 1966, 1974–1975), for example, has found that some (but not all) parents teach children letter names and perhaps letter shapes, but this does not typically extend to explicit instruction in areas such as phonemic awareness. It is possible, of course, that children do gain such knowledge incidentally from these activities, but this falls far short of the sort of instruction prescribed by those who believe in formal teaching of the alphabetic principle.

One such study, McGee, Lomax, and Head (1988), examined the way in which young children read not only environmental print signs and labels, but also "functional" print, defined as the types of text found in the home (e.g., a grocery list, a telephone book, a coupon) not associated with specific logos, pictures, or symbols. This latter category would more likely include print that is what we defined above as "properly specified"—that is, print within a context that gives the reader some background information to reduce the number of possible meanings, but that does not completely eliminate uncertainty and thus requires some attention to the actual text. McGee and her colleagues interviewed eighty-one children, ages three to five, attending preschool and kindergarten classes. Using a detailed coding scheme, they determined what children could read from both functional and environmental categories of text, and what details they attended to in attempting to comprehend the text in question. Children were classified by whether they could read eleven or more isolated words from a list ("expert"), one to ten words ("novice"), or no words ("nonword"). All the words were drawn from beginning-reader books.

Little difference was found in the percentage of children among the three categories who could read the environmental print example presented to the children, confirming that this is probably the first type of print that children attend to, but not one that leads immediately to independent reading. However, the expert readers attempted to read the functional print items at a much higher rate (79 percent) than the novice (51 percent) or nonword readers (28 percent). This is an indication that functional print may be the next step along a developmental path taken by some early readers. It may be, that is, that children encountering written language may move from very "contextualized" environmental print, with its visual information to help determine the meaning, to the less contextualized functional print, with its familiar uses but smaller number of extralinguistic clues.

Even some of the nonword and novice readers who made attempts to read the functional items did so by attending to the text itself (the "graphic detail"), not just the surrounding symbols or drawings on the page. While McGee (1986) later commented that the percentage of nonword readers who attended to the specifics of the text (16 percent) was low, an alternative explanation is that there exists a gradual developmental sequence in early readers as they acquire knowledge about text. All this is consistent with our hypothesis that knowledge about print may grow slowly as exposure to text increases, eventually leading to the ability to read independently.[6]

Further evidence that children seem to grow in their knowledge of written language comes from a study by Lomax and McGee (1987). Here the researchers tested children ages three to seven on a variety of measures, including their "concepts about print" (e.g., knowing which side of the book is up or that the print moves from left to right), their awareness of the sounds letters make and how words can be broken apart into smaller, "phonemic" units (such as the example of "cat" as "cuh" "ah" and "tuh"), and their ability to read simple words presented in isolation. Lomax and McGee's results, partially summarized in Table 3.1, show that some awareness of environmental and functional print as well as letter-sound correspondence exists even among very young children.

Environmental print awareness is one of the first stages of literacy acquisition for these children, with three-year-olds identifying nearly two-thirds of the environmental print words when presented in context. Awareness of functional print items is also present at an early age, and more importantly, continues to increase up through the time children begin formal schooling. Substantial increases in letter-sound correspondence knowledge and phonemic awareness occur between ages three and four and four and five. The ability to read words in isolation, indicating acquisition of the alphabetic principle, is not seen at all until age five, however.

One interpretation of these trends in the data shown in Table 3.1 is that exposure to print leads to gradual acquisition of the two components of Share's (1995) definition of the alphabetic principle, phonemic awareness and letter-sound corre-

Table 3.1
Growth in Print Knowledge Over Time

ITEM	TOTAL POSSIBLE	AGE 3	AGE 4	AGE 5	AGE 6
Environmental Print (in context)	20	73.5% (14.70)	87.2% (17.44)	93.8% (18.75)	97.8% (19.56)
Functional Print	40	35.8% (14.30)	56.8% (22.70)	75.3% (30.10)	81.4% (32.56)
Phonemic Awareness (initial sound)	20	20% (4.00)	58.7% (11.74)	86.5% (17.30)	95% (19.00)
Letter Sounds	21	21.2% (4.45)	53.8% (11.13)	87.5% (17.50)	97.2% (20.44)
Word List	100	.05% (.05)	.83% (.83)	27.2% (27.15)	75.4% (75.39)

(adapted from Lomax & McGee, 1987; Table 2, p. 246)

spondence, which in turn leads children to acquire the "insight" that can be used to recode words in isolation.[7] Indeed, Lomax and McGee (1987) found through a sophisticated statistical procedure (structural equation modeling analysis) that their data were consistent with a developmental path.

Conclusion

Serious problems exist with the evidence cited to show that children cannot acquire the alphabetic principle without formal instruction. First, researchers have failed to take into account the fact that environmental print is generally overspecified. Because children can derive the necessary meaning of many logos and signs without attending to the text, reception of this input does not necessarily lead to any acquisition of specific features of the writing system. Other forms of written input, or environmental print that is more properly specified, would appear to be needed to make the text more salient and comprehensible.

Although it may not always lead directly to independent reading, environmental print does serve a function in helping children learn to read. As Goodman (1986) and others have noted, children begin to see that written language has a purpose and meaning, even if they are not paying close attention to the "graphic" detail of the letters and words embedded in it. The evidence is consistent with the hypothesis that acquisition is a process beginning with environmental and functional print, moving through stages of greater attention to graphic detail in an attempt to comprehend texts. This acquired knowledge of print and the way it functions appears to lead ultimately to the ability to read some words independently in context and, finally, in isolation.

More research is needed on precisely what types of exposure help children acquire initial literacy. Snow and her colleagues (Snow & Goldfield, 1982, 1983; Snow & Ninio, 1986) conducted a series of studies on the discourse of "storybook" reading between children and parents, and Yaden (Smolkin et al., 1988; Yaden et al., 1989; Yaden, 1988) has looked at the types of elaborative questions children ask during storybook reading sessions. Both of these sets of studies give us some insight into the nature of adult's assistance to pre-readers. Little is known on precisely what types of elaborative assistance or contextual help beginning readers acquire certain aspects of text. Possible exceptions to this gap in the research are Ehri's studies on fingerpointing-reading (Ehri and Sweet, 1991) and Samuels' earlier work (Samuels, 1967) on illustrations and isolated word learning, but neither of these are necessarily representative of normal print exposure for early readers.

A second problem encountered in the evidence on acquiring the alphabetic principle was the unrealistic estimations of the quantity and duration of input that are likely to be needed to acquire the information contained in the input. The very short exposures used in most training studies, some no more than a few minutes, and the extremely impoverished input (a few words) are not likely to lead to any easily measurable acquisition of linguistic information, and are completely inadequate to test whether children can acquire such information from exposure alone. Research from oral language (Pinker, 1994) and other aspects of written language acquisition (Nagy, Herman, & Anderson, 1985) suggest that many aspects of the language are acquired over time, often over a period of years, not minutes. This of course places severe limitations on the type of evidence available to answer this question, since it is almost impossible to observe children carefully over long periods of time to see what sort of assistance they might receive when learning to read.

It should be again emphasized that our alternative interpretation of the available evidence, like Share's (1995) version, is still very much open to debate. This is due in part to the nature of the phenomenon being studied. The naturalistic inquiry required to determine if print exposure can lead to the alphabetic insight by necessity lacks the experimental control needed to give us a clean test of the hypothesis. Strong claims that systematic, explicit metalinguistic instruction is necessary (versus merely helpful) for children to learn how to read are not warranted by the data currently available, however.

4

Age and Reading

Children can learn to read at different ages, in different settings, and with different forms of adult assistance. In this chapter, we will examine additional evidence from a variety of sources on how learning to read is accomplished through appropriate exposure to comprehensible written language, with the help of both elaborative and, on occasion, some metalinguistic instruction. Much of this evidence comes from children learning to read outside the classroom and, as such, has its limitations. One cannot always be certain of the types of help children are given outside of school, yet the data we will discuss here is at least suggestive that elaborative assistance and access to print may be more important in assuring long-term reading success than other factors. I will begin by reviewing the research on "early readers," children who learn to read before arriving at school; next, I will analyze several studies on the relationship between the age children learn to read and their long-term reading proficiency; and finally, I will discuss some of the potential pitfalls of programs that focus on instruction versus access in helping struggling readers.

"Natural" and Precocious Readers

The issue of whether children need systematic metalinguistic training in order to learn how to read can be addressed in part through several case studies that have been published on "natural" readers. Goodman and Goodman (1982), for example, reported that their daughter Kay learned to read on her own, and at age six-and-a-half could read at a fifth-grade level on a standardized measure of reading. They report that their daughter began reading "with no instruction" independently at the age of five years, six months. Despite a lack of formal teaching, Kay's reading did not come without what we have termed elaborative support from her parents. Her environment was "rich in language experience. She has always been read to, listened to, and talked to. Singing, poetry, nursery rhymes, and oral family language games are daily fare in her home" (p. 221).

Torrey (1969) investigated the case of John, who learned to read without any adult instruction at age five. John's mother, who had a tenth-grade education, reported that no one had "read to or taught him" to read. He did, however, watch a great deal of television, where many children's shows had objects labeled. Torrey notes that John was not pressured by his parents into reading. His exposure to sufficiently specified print—in games and on television—was apparently sufficient to allow him to begin reading independently. Forester (1977) cites the cases of two girls, a five-year-old and four-year-old, both of whom learned to read without instruction. The five-year-old began reading after her grandmother gave her a common form of elaborative assistance: reading to her. The four-year-old began reading after listening to tape recordings of children's books. Forester notes that the children took "obvious pleasure" from their reading (p. 164).

Case study and survey evidence on learning to read without formal instruction is also found in the research on "precocious" readers, usually defined as those children who are reading at a high level (at second- or third-grade level) upon entering first grade. The earliest reports of such readers date back to the first part of this century (reviewed in Coltheart, 1979; and Torrey, 1979). More recently, Henderson, Jackson, and Mukamal (1993) reported on the case of Max, a young boy who learned to read without formal instruction at the age of three. As in the case of John discussed above, Max seemed to benefit from early television viewing in learning letters and words. His parents report that after watching the television game show *Wheel of Fortune,* Max appeared to know the names of many letters and could read certain labels on food packages at the age of one year, nine months. When Max was two, his mother began offering some metalinguistic assistance by using letter magnets to spell words out for him on the refrigerator related to kitchen activities. His mother also started to write short stories for Max about the day's events and read these to him, in addition to reading regular storybooks to him twice a day.

Survey studies confirm that a certain number of children learn to read without school instruction. Durkin (1966) conducted two studies in which she examined 49 precocious readers in California and 30 in New York. In the California study, Durkin found that more than half of the children received only occasional instruction from parents and/or siblings in learning to read, although all of the parents reported that they read to their children. Being read to was also the most important factor indicated by the children themselves as motivating them to learn how to read. Similar results were found in the New York study, where all of the parents of early readers reported reading to their children. My own research based on data collected from a more representative sample of United States parents has found that perhaps as many as one out of every ten children begins reading outside of school (McQuillan, in press: a), suggesting the phenomenon may not be as rare as previously thought.

Jackson, Donaldson, and Mills (1991, cited in Jackson & Lu, 1992) studied 116 children who were reading at a third-grade level or higher upon entering first grade, including some children whose first language was not English (Jackson & Lu, 1992). King and Friesen (1972) found 31 children who were reading upon entry into kindergarten. Some of these children undoubtedly learned to read with adult assistance, but there is no evidence that they did so with any systematic, formal instruction usually associated with school—phonics training, phonemic awareness exercises, and other skill-building activities.

Some common characteristics have been identified in the backgrounds of these precocious readers. First, as Jackson (1988) comments, parents of precocious readers "rarely give the impression of having pushed children toward goals that the children did not share" (p. 203); that is, children were not pressured to read before they felt ready. Second, precocious readers were usually given extensive elaborative assistance by being read to by their parents (Jackson, 1988; Plessas & Oakes, 1964; Teale, 1978; Torrey, 1979). Of course, these same activities may have led to the phonological insights that are thought by some to be critical to learning to read (Goswami & Bryant, 1990). Evidence also exists that early readers receive certain simple types of metalinguistic assistance, such as learning the names of letters (Briggs & Elkind, 1977), but this, again, seems to be much less extensive than the systematic instruction typically advocated for early literacy instruction. The case of Max reported in Henderson et al. (1988) may be an instance of this, where watching a letter-game on T.V. and having his mother spell words for him was sufficient assistance to allow him to recode. But since this assistance occurred within the context of considerable elaborative help, it is difficult to say whether it was necessary or merely helpful. Third, early readers come from environments where they saw how text conveyed meaning, including seeing adults who engaged in reading and being continually exposed to new books in the home (Brenna, 1995). Finally, early readers usually show a strong desire to read and like to read independently for pleasure (Forester, 1977; Brenna, 1995). Given proper conditions of a supportive environment, some children clearly can and do learn to read without being explicitly taught in formal settings, and in many cases, with little assistance other than being given easy access to print and being read to by others.[1]

All this is not to say that *all* children would be equally successful in similar environments with abundant print access and elaborative assistance to help make texts comprehensible. But the option should at least be considered. Poor readers often receive significantly less exposure to print and instead are given intensive metalinguistic assistance in remedial programs (Allington, 1983), in some sense the opposite of what successful readers experience. As we will learn in the next chapter, these attempts to offer large amounts of metalinguistic assistance have had only modest results in improving real reading, and there is still little evidence that even these modest gains are long-term.

Age of Learning to Read and Later Reading Achievement

While it is clear that some young children can and do learn to read without formal instruction, there remains the related question of whether learning to read by a certain age *per se* provides children with longer-term benefits in reading achievement. Two types of research design have been used in studies that attempt to answer this question. It is important to distinguish between the two and the kind of information each design can give us. The first type is a nonexperimental, "static group" design (Campbell & Stanley, 1966), where the researchers take a group of children already reading by the age of school entry and compare them to a group of children who are nonreaders. The two groups' reading scores are then compared over a period of years in order to determine the effects of the age at which reading began on eventual reading achievement.

Nonexperimental Designs

At least four studies have made such comparisons, and all four have found that early readers maintain their advantage over nonreaders into the later years. Durkin's (1966) investigation, discussed above, of 30 early readers and 30 nonreaders at school entry found that the early readers were still reading at a higher grade level than their first-grade nonreader classmates in the third grade.

Sutton (1969) found similar results with a group of 46 early readers and 59 nonreaders; the early readers were still better by grade three, although she did not analyze her data for statistical significance. Morrison, Harris, and Auerbach (1971) looked at 58 early reading first graders in New York, all of whom outscored the nonreader first-grade children through the third grade. The differences in reading comprehension at grade three were significant.

Tobin and Pikulski (1988) tracked a group of early readers and nonreaders through grade six, and reported that the early readers continued to score significantly higher than the nonreaders in a number of standardized measures. At the end of sixth grade, the early readers did better on the Gates-MacGinitie Reading Tests (total reading mean scores: early reader = 630.8 [40.1], regular readers = 582.6 [37.2]; calculated effect size from test statistic = 1.2), as well as on informal measures of oral reading, reading speed, mean instructional level, silent reading, and comprehension questions. All of these differences were statistically significant with moderate to large effect sizes.

There is a problem with using the evidence provided in these studies, however. When using static group comparisons, a risk exists that factors other than the one being studied may account for the differences between the two groups. In the case of the early readers, it may be that some factor other than the age at which they began to read is the cause of the difference between reading scores in the later grades.

A closer examination of the early reader groups in the studies reviewed above reveals the presence of such factors. In Durkin (1966), for example, four of the five selected case studies of one early reader group found that their homes had a large number of books. Since exposure and access to print is a strong predictor of eventual literacy development (Krashen, 1993), it is likely that the continued gains made by these early readers is attributable to the environment of the home over the years studied, and not to the age they began reading *per se*. Sutton reported that the median level of the father's schooling in her early reader group was 15 years, compared to 12 years for the nonreader fathers. Morrow (1983) found that children in the homes of better-educated parents showed more interest in books and had more books in the home. While education is only a rough proxy for the print environment in the home, it is at least plausible that the early reader/nonreader groups differed in their access to books. Tobin and Pilulski (1988) and Morrison, Harris, and Auerbach (1971) provided no data on the home print environment of their subjects, but given the evidence on the literacy backgrounds of other early readers noted by Jackson (1988) and Plessas and Oakes (1964) above, it again seems reasonable to suppose that there were differences in access between their groups as well which help account for the long-term success of the early readers, rather than attributing this to the age at which they began to read.

Experimental and Quasi-Experimental Designs

A second and more reliable study design is an experimental or quasi-experimental one, where children are (ideally) assigned randomly to two groups, or at least matched according to certain important variables. One group receives early instruction in reading and one does not. In this way we can see whether the age at which reading begins itself is responsible for the long-term differences in reading development. Table 4.1 summarizes the results of four such studies, all of which found that the gains made by readers who begin to read "early" are short term in nature and/or have little to no long-lasting effects on reading proficiency. Since each study used different standardized measures and reported their results with different sample statistics, I have converted the data, when available, into effect sizes to make a more general comparison of the results (Light & Pillemer, 1984). Effect sizes allow us to compare findings of the studies using a common metric.

In Bradley's (1956) study, two groups of 31 first graders were matched on several measures, including the father's socioeconomic status. One group received instruction at the beginning of first grade, according to normal school practice. The second group was divided into three subgroups according to what the teacher determined was their "reading readiness." These three groups began to receive reading instruction when the teacher believed them ready; the first subgroup at five months after school entry, the second at eight months, and the third at ten months after school entry. The early reader group did better during the initial tests given two months into grade two, but those differences disappeared by the ninth month of that same school year, with the "delayed" readers actually doing slightly better at the end of grades two and three. Note in Table 4.1 that the effect size of the early reading treatment declines steadily throughout the three years, from +1.8 to −.67.

Gray and Klaus (1970) studied 61 at-risk children who were randomly assigned to three groups: One group participated in a ten-week summer reading and reading readiness program each of the three summers prior to the group's entry into first grade, another group attended summer school two summers prior to first grade, and the third group received no special instruction. The differences among the three groups were significant only in the second grade, with the control group doing a bit better than both groups in the first grade and actually outscoring the group that re-

Table 4.1
Experimental Studies of Early Readers

STUDY	GRADE READING SCORES MEASURED[a]	SIGNIFICANT DIFFERENCE FAVORING EARLY READERS?	EFFECT SIZE[b]
Bradley (1956)	November, 2nd	Yes	+1.8
	June, 2nd	No	−.06
	June, 3rd	No	−.67
Gray and Klaus (1970)	June, 1st	No	n/a
	June, 2nd	Yes	n/a
	June, 3rd	No	n/a
Durkin (1974–1975)[c]	September, 1st	Yes	+.86
	March, 2nd	Yes	+.59
	March, 3rd	No	+.34
	March, 4th	No	+.50
Hanson and Farrell (1995)	Fall, 12th	Yes	+.10

[a] Standardized reading comprehension scores were used for all studies.
[b] "+" favors early reader group. Effect sizes were determined according to formulas provided by Wolf (1986) from the sample statistic used in the original study.
[c] Effect size calculated from the mean reading raw scores reported by Durkin.

ceived the earliest instruction in all three grades. It should be noted, however, that despite the early intervention, there is no indication that the experimental group was actually reading by the beginning of first grade, and therefore may not have been a true case of early readers.

Durkin (1974–1975) compared two groups (total of 33) of four-year-olds randomly assigned to two treatment groups, one that received special reading and reading readiness instruction, and one that attended a normal kindergarten program. Her six-year study showed that while the early reader group did better in the first and second grades, no significant differences were present by grades three and four. While the early reader group still outscored the nonreader group at the end of the study, the advantage was marginal, with the effect sizes exhibiting an overall declining trend as the children got older.

Finally, Hanson and Farrell (1995) looked at a large sample (n = 3,959) of high school seniors, about two-thirds of whom had participated in a kindergarten early-reading program. The experimental program, the Beginning Reading Program (BRP), was carried out during the school year 1972–73 in 24 of the 25 school districts that took part in the longitudinal study. The researchers gave measures of reading comprehension to all those who were high school seniors in these same districts.

The combination of those students from the non-BRP district plus those students who transferred into the BRP districts after kindergarten gave the experimenters a control group with whom to compare the students who learned to read in the BRP program. The design of the study was posttest only—that is, only the reading scores from grade twelve were used to compare the possible effects of the BRP treatment—and assignment of the students to either the experimental or control groups was, of course, not random. Hanson and Farrell found that those students who were in the BRP program scored significantly higher than those who were not ($F = 6.2$ [degrees of freedom not given], $p < .001$).

While the large number of subjects made the difference in mean scores statistically significant, the difference in performance between the early and regular reading groups was actually quite small, with an effect size of only .10, making the practical significance of the results questionable. There are also some plausible reasons for the difference in scores that may help account for even this slight advantage attributed to the early reading program. Those districts that elected to use the BRP may have other institutional qualities besides the kindergarten program that may have affected reading performance, such as better reading programs at the upper levels and/or better libraries that in turn could have affected senior high reading scores. It seems likely that districts that self-selected into the BRP project made other special efforts to assist students' reading performance compared to those districts that did not participate in the BRP, making any claims about the effects of the kindergarten program on long-term results, at the very least, somewhat suspect.

From the above studies there appears to exist what we may term a "Tortoise and Hare Effect" for age and learning to read: Children who learn to read early in experimental studies do better starting out, but the gains made are negligible and insignificant by as early as the third grade. This is consistent with cross-national comparisons that examine age of initial reading instruction and later achievement. Reporting on data from a cross-national comparison of reading, Elley (1992) states that countries that begin reading instruction at ages five and six have some initial advantages, but that those children who began "late" as seven-year-olds have usually caught up by age nine. It is important to note that those countries included in Elley's survey that delayed instruction until age seven were economically well-off and reported an ample supply of books in the home, suggesting that access to print, not age, is the critical ingredient in achievement (Krashen & McQuillan, 1996).

Early Reading and Later Success

While learning to read by a certain age is not in and of itself critical, there *is* a relationship between the level of reading performance in first grade and later years. Several studies (Juel, 1988; Lundberg, Frost, & Petersen, 1988; Shaywitz et al., 1995) have found that children who are poor readers in the early years tend to be poor readers in later grades (up to grade six in one study). These studies use "static group" designs, however, and as such are not able to isolate age of independent reading as critical to long-term development. What the evidence reviewed here suggests is that learning to read before a certain age, all other factors being equal, does not *in and of itself* confer any lasting advantages in later grades.[2]

The logic of early "intervention" or programs aimed specifically to raise reading scores seems to be that if a child is put at grade level early, he will be able to "stay up" with school reading and will read for pleasure in the quantity needed for normal vocabulary and comprehension growth. The reading problem, that is to say, is essentially located within the child (and indicates a lack of metalinguistic knowledge). At the very least it is thought that changing the child is necessary, perhaps even sufficient, to maintaining long-term reading success. If, however, many (most?) reading difficulties are *not* within the child, but are due rather to a lack of access to comprehensible reading materials in a supportive environment, then bringing a child up to grade level her first year of schooling will do little in the long run. As we will see in Chapter 7, poor readers are very often in precisely this situation. By the time remediated readers are in the middle grades, they may very well be back to (relatively) low levels of achievement. Unfortunately, such longitudinal research in education is rare, and we have relatively little data to go on in judging the long-term success of most intervention programs.[3] Krashen's (1997a) analysis of studies on the long-term effects of phonemic awareness training studies show that early metalinguistic training does not, in fact, lead to sustained gains in later grades. To be sure, more information is needed on the longitudinal effects of early intervention, especially if a significant amount of resources are to be devoted to it.

5

Sound and Reading

The confusion over the role of "phonics" in reading has never been greater, both in the popular press and the scientific literature. On the one hand, some researchers have claimed that training children in "phonemic awareness" and sound-letter correspondences are critical to reading success (e.g., Share, 1995). Frank Smith, on the other hand, in his classic volume *Psycholinguistics and Reading* (1973), called the supposed importance of sound in reading "the Great Fallacy." What do the sounds of letters have to do with reading? Is knowing how sounds go together in spoken speech critical in learning how to read? What does the relationship between such "phonological awareness" and reading ability mean for learning how to read? These are some of the issues we will address in this chapter.

What Can Sound Do for You?

We noted in Chapter 2 that knowing the sounds that letters make, whether garnered through metalinguistic instruction or the experience of being exposed to print, is one of the things we can use to make sense of text. Knowing how sounds are linked to letters can help a reader figure out the meaning of a word by reducing the possibilities of what an unknown word could be. For example, if a child is reading a story about a lion, and comes across the unknown word *lair*, knowing what sound the letter *l* usually makes at the beginning of the word allows him to reduce the number of possibilities, eliminating such possibilities as *cage* or *house*. This knowledge of sound-letter correspondence may be even more useful when you have been given few or no clues provided by other parts of the text, as is the case when a reader encounters unknown words in a list of random words, or, as is done in many studies, is given a made-up or nonsense word.

Yet this is very different from saying, as has been done by several researchers, that knowledge of how sounds relate to letters, or how words can be broken down into their constituent parts or "phonemes" in speech, is a *central* process in reading, either at the early stages or for fluent reading. Part of the confusion arises from the mistaken belief that somehow speech is immediately and instantaneously "decodable" into meaning, that the mere sounds of spoken speech are directly connected to a word's meaning. This is, as Goodman (1971) noted long ago, false: Both speech and writing are "codes" and neither is immediately or intrinsically related to the meaning they convey. Both the sounds of speech and the letters of written language are "surface" structures of language, which we assign rather arbitrarily to concepts or meaning. Thus, converting letters to sounds—often referred to as "decoding"—is not sufficient to allow text to make sense. Meaning must still be brought to the spoken word every bit as much as the written word.

In fact, most words cannot be decoded letter by letter with any accuracy without having some idea beforehand of the word you are trying to pronounce. At least a rough guess at the meaning of a word is often needed to pronounce any given letter with accuracy. Try to pronounce the beginning of this word:

r————————————————e————————————————c . . .

Did you pronounce the e long as in *recent* or short as in *recommend?* Is the c pronounced hard as in *recluse* or soft as in *receive?* You would need to know the rest of the word to make such decisions, which means already having some idea of what the word is. Knowing how letters are pronounced can help reduce the possibilities, but it typically cannot do the job alone.[1]

This logical problem with the use of sound in reading goes to the heart of the often-heard practical rationale for "phonological processing," that if you've heard a word but haven't seen it in print, then "recoding" it from print to sound would be very helpful. In fact, at best we usually only use our knowledge of the sounds that letters or clusters of letters make for eliminating possibilities, rather than identifying precise pronunciations. Children and adults do not, in fact, typically attempt to decode every word to sound when they read, as demonstrated by a series of studies by Ken and Yetta Goodman and their colleagues (see Gollash, 1982; Goodman, 1996). Readers often make "miscues" or mistakes that make sense in the context of the passage they are reading, because they are focused on meaning first and foremost (see also Weaver, 1994, for a discussion of miscues in reading).

Some Empirical Evidence on Sound in Reading

Several researchers, such as Stanovich (1986, 1993) and McGuinness (1997), have attempted to argue that knowing certain elements in the relationship between sound and written language is critical to fluent reading and to learning how to read. An enormous number of studies have been conducted and continue to be published guided by these assumptions, and recently, reading policy in many states (notably California) are quite literally dictated by them. Does recent evidence on the role of phonological processes in reading contradict Goodman's and Smith's Model?

The Goodman-Smith view of reading predicts that knowledge of sound-letter correspondence will make a small contribution to beginning reading, since those who have such knowledge will be able to use it to help them figure out unknown words, as in the "lair" example given above. In the following sections, I will argue that the evidence to date is still consistent with that view. Since the number of studies on the topic of sound and reading are far greater than the amount of space available here, only some of the key claims made, along with a few illustrative studies, will be discussed.[2]

Good Readers Have Better Phonological Processing Than Poor Readers

One type of evidence thought to disprove the Goodman-Smith Model is the well-established finding that good readers tend to have better sound or "phonological" awareness than poor readers (Stanovich, 1993). Good readers, for example, are usually better than poor readers at pronouncing "nonsense" or made-up words (e.g., *grack* or *wug*), performing "phoneme deletion" tasks (i.e., pronounce a word with certain sounds deleted, such as *trick* without the *r* sound), and similar artificial word games. Thus, it has been argued, phonological factors must be critical in reading, or at least in distinguishing good readers from poor readers.

Good readers, without question, typically do better than poor readers on many of these phonological tests. Juel's (1988) study of good and poor readers in fourth grade provides a clear case of this, as shown in Table 5.1. Poor readers scored significantly lower than good readers on tests not only of "real" reading (reading comprehension), but also on a test that focused on sounding out words, or decoding. Suppose, however, that phonological abilities were themselves largely a product of reading and reading experience. These same correlational findings between phonological ability and reading would be equally consistent with the data. As Krashen (1998b) has observed, the relationship could also be as shown in Figure 5.1, referring specifically to the type of phonological skills considered most critical by many researchers, phonemic awareness.

In Chapter 3 we reviewed some of the evidence supportive of this relationship: Children begin with certain concepts about print through exposure to comprehensible written language (environmental print), then begin to identify words in properly specified contexts, and eventually develop phonemic awareness of the sort that allows them to "decode" real words out of context or the nonsense words used to detect phonological processing abilities. If this relationship is correct, then the superior

Table 5.1
Reading Comprehension Scores and Decoding Ability of Fourth-Grade Readers

	GOOD READERS	POOR READERS
Reading Comprehension	5.9	3.5
Decoding	42.6	28.2

(from Juel, 1988, Table 1, p. 441)

Figure 5.1
The Relationship Between Reading Experience and Phonemic Awareness

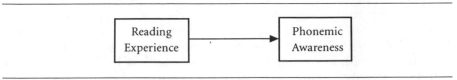

phonemic awareness of good readers is not necessarily causal: Phonemic and other forms of phonological awareness, as well as a good deal of sound-letter correspondence knowledge, may largely be the result of experience with print. This knowledge may then be helpful to some children once they begin reading, since knowing the sound properties of print may in turn make some text more comprehensible (again, as in the "lair" example above). Thus studies that find better readers have better phonemic awareness could just as well be interpreted in favor of the Goodman-Smith view of reading and may largely be the result of experience with print.

Phonemic Awareness Predicts Reading Growth

In addition to studies that have found good readers to have better phonemic awareness than poor readers, there have been longitudinal studies that have found that children's level of phonemic awareness in early grades is sometimes (but not always) related to reading success in later grades. Juel, Griffith, and Gough (1986), for example, found that a measure of phonemic awareness in October of first grade correlated moderately ($r = .56$) with a measure of second-grade reading comprehension. But this staggered or "cross-lagged" correlational evidence (relating performance on a test at one point in time with performance on another test several months or years later) does not necessarily indicate that the strength of phonemic awareness in kindergarten or first grade is the *cause* of higher levels of reading comprehension in later grades, as has often been concluded. This same evidence is also consistent with the notion that reading experience is the primary source of both reading ability and certain types of phonemic awareness for many readers.

We have hypothesized that phonemic awareness is largely a product of reading experience, and that reading experience is a consequence of a "print-rich" environment, one in which reading materials are easily accessible. It stands to reason that children who have more exposure to written language in, say, the first grade, resulting in higher levels of phonemic awareness, are also going to have higher levels of print exposure and reading experience in subsequent grades, resulting in both more phonemic awareness and better reading comprehension in later years. This assumes, of course, that phonemic awareness is always or typically correlated with higher reading ability. As we shall see, this is not always the case. At times, the size of the relationship between reading ability and phonemic awareness appears to be rather modest among some readers, again indicating that phonemic awareness may be neither a critical element in reading achievement nor a cause of reading acquisition.

Reading with Poor Phonemic Awareness?

From the evidence above, it would appear that many forms of phonemic awareness do not develop prior to alphabetic reading. It is also possible to find children and adults who are good readers in English but have low levels of phonemic awareness. For some researchers, these concepts appear contradictory: A good reader is in part very often *defined* as one having good phonemic awareness. But if we use the term "good reader" in the everyday sense, as one who can understand a passage of appropriate difficulty, then there is indeed evidence that one can be a good reader with poor phonemic awareness.

Bruck (1990), for example, found a subgroup of adults who had normal reading comprehension levels but poor phonemic awareness. As shown in Table 5.2, these "dyslexics" did just fine in reading comprehension but poorly on isolated or nonsense word tasks. They committed ten times as many errors on nonsense word pronunciation, and were nearly three times more inaccurate in one task of isolated word identification. Yet they could *read*—in the meaningful sense of the word—just fine.

Similar findings for adult "dyslexics" were found by Elbro, Nielsen, and Petersen (1994). Their sample of adult dyslexics scored no worse than an age-equivalent group on reading comprehension accuracy (97.7 percent vs. 98.8 percent) but significantly lower on tests of nonsense word reading (67.5 percent vs. 95.9 percent accuracy). The only difference in real reading found was in speed: The "dyslexics" were slightly slower readers than the controls, a finding that is consistent with the results of a study of "dyslexic" medical students by Banks, Guyer, and Guyer (1995).

Children who are good comprehenders but poor "decoders" have also been studied (Stothard & Hulme, 1996). Some children who are high in phonemic awareness have been found to be low in reading comprehension; some show the opposite pattern. Marshall and Cossu have also conducted several studies of both children and adults who have normal reading comprehension (or comparable to controls) but show virtually no ability to perform phonemic awareness tasks, including both "hyperlexics" and children with Down's Syndrome (Marshall & Cossu, 1991; Cossu, Rossini, & Marshall, 1993; see also Campbell, 1991). All this leads to the conclusion

Table 5.2
"Dyslexic" and Normal College Readers

	"DYSLEXIC" READERS	NORMAL READERS
Reading Comprehension (Percentile)	76	79
Nonsense Word Pronunciation Errors	11.71	1.7
High Frequency/Exception Isolated Word Identification (Error Rate)	1.57	.45

(from Bruck, 1990, Tables 1, 2, 3, and 7)

that real reading—reading passages for comprehension—is not to be confused with its sometime correlate—phonemic awareness.

Children Need to Be Trained in Phonemic Awareness

Currently massive efforts are being made in many states to "train" students in phonemic awareness in the hopes that this will produce appreciable gains in long-term reading scores. California has led the way with some of the most drastic changes in curriculum and funding to promote such efforts (e.g., California Reading Task Force Report, 1995). It is by no means clear, however, that these efforts will pay off, judging from the current research evidence.

Training Appears to Have Strong Effects on Phonemic Awareness, Weak Effects on Real Reading

It is important to keep in mind that the goal of reading instruction is to improve what we normally associate with reading—comprehension of passages. As noted above, reading comprehension and phonemic awareness do not always go hand and hand. It is not surprising to find, then, that studies in which children are explicitly trained in phonemic awareness make huge leaps in phonemic awareness, but often only modest to small gains in reading comprehension. Krashen (1997a, 1998a), for example, computed effect sizes for four frequently cited studies of phonemic awareness training (Ball & Blachman, 1991; Cunningham, 1990; Lie, 1991; Lundberg, Frost, & Petersen, 1988), and found that while the gains in phonemic awareness were large (effect sizes .88 to 2.26), the impact on reading comprehension was modest (effect sizes ranging from .28 to .57). Even these gains on "reading" are probably somewhat inflated, given that three of the four studies Krashen analyzed used reading measures consisting, in whole or in part, of individual isolated words. Lundberg et al. (1988), for example, which is widely cited as showing the superior effects of phonemic awareness training, used a 400 isolated word–picture matching test as a measure of real reading, not connected text or passage comprehension. Cunningham (1990) used three combined measures to test reading, including at the primer and primary levels measures of "sound-symbol correspondence, word recognition, and reading comprehension" (p. 432), so it is difficult to say how the training affected reading comprehension *per se*. Ball and Blachman (1991) used only isolated word identification tasks. Lie (1991) was the only study to use a test measuring exclusively the comprehension of connected text.

Other phonemic awareness studies find no gains in any measure of real reading, even when the amount of training is substantial. Torgesen and Hecht (1996), for example, report on the first year of a five-year project comparing different types of skills training for children identified as having low scores on phoneme deletion and letter-naming tasks in kindergarten. Each treatment group received 80 minutes of one-on-one tutorials each week during kindergarten and first grade. The children were randomly assigned (n = 200) to one of four groups, including an "embedded

Table 5.3

Comparison of Phonemic Awareness Training Groups

	NO TRAINING	TUTORIAL GROUP	PA & SYNTHETIC PHONICS	EMBEDDED PHONICS
Blend Phonemes	11.4 (5.4)	13.0 (5.5)	14.9 (3.6)	13.1 (4.0)
Word Attack	2.6 (3.5)	5.8 (6.7)	9.6 (7.8)	5.4 (5.1)
Reading Comprehension	7.3 (6.7)	11.4 (7.1)	10.7 (7.5)	9.6 (6.5)

(from Torgeson & Hecht, 1996, Table 6.1, p. 151)

phonics," "phonological awareness (PA) plus synthetic phonics," regular tutorial group (no explicit phonemic awareness training), and a control group. At the end of first grade, tests of various phonological abilities (blending phonemes together, deleting phonemes, and pronouncing nonsense words ["word attack"]) and reading comprehension were administered. Table 5.3 includes selected results.

Consistent with other phonemic awareness training studies, the Phonemic Awareness–trained groups performed substantially better than the No Training group on phonemic awareness tests, but *not* on reading comprehension. In the word attack test, the effect size for the Phonological Awareness plus Synthetic Phonics group versus the No Training group is large (2.0). However, note that on other phonemic awareness measures, such as the "blend phonemes" task, the difference between the PA plus Synthetic Phonics group and the No Training students was not as great (14.9 versus 11.4, effect size = .83). For reading comprehension, the difference between the two groups was not even statistically significant. It is also interesting to note that the No Training group received no tutorial help in kindergarten or first grade, yet seemed to be progressing in at least some aspects of phonemic awareness without instruction, as in other studies (Juel, 1988).

What is most important about these results is that there were no significant differences among the treatment groups on any of the five measures other than the word attack test. That is, those groups of children who received large doses of explicit, systematic phonemic awareness training did no better on most tasks than those who received no training at all in phonemic awareness. Most disappointing is the fact that none of the children who received extensive tutoring did significantly better in reading comprehension than the control children, who received no help at all.

Even in those few studies where phonemic awareness does have an effect, the gains appear to be short-lived. Byrne and Fielding-Barnsley (1993) tracked a group of children who had received 12 weeks of phonemic awareness training in kindergarten for a one-year period. By the time the children were in first grade, there were no differences between the trained and untrained groups on isolated word identification or spelling, and only a small advantage for the previously trained group in nonsense word reading.

Table 5.4

Growth of Phonemic Awareness (Segmentation) Among Seven-Year-Olds
(Pre- to Posttest Gain Scores)

	TRAINED GROUP (PHONOLOGY ONLY)	UNTRAINED GROUP (READING ONLY)
Sound Deletion	9.90	3.25
Nonsense Word Segmentation	7.23	5.81
Sound Blending	6.86	4.74
Sound Categorization	3.67	3.09

(from Hatcher et al., 1994, p. 49, Table 2)

Phonemic Awareness Grows without Instruction

Little question exists that certain aspects of phonological awareness grow on their own without any explicit, metalinguistic instruction, and that this growth appears to be largely a result of reading itself. Hatcher, Hulme, and Ellis (1994) report the results of a longitudinal study of a group of seven-year-olds placed in various instructional treatment groups for 30–40 minute sessions each day over a 20-week period, ranging from "reading alone" to "phonology alone." Consistent with the studies analyzed by Krashen (1997a), those children who received *no* instruction in phonemic awareness got better, as seen in Table 5.4.

Despite the fact that they received no formal instruction in phonemic awareness, the reading group made clear gains in all areas of phonological awareness and processing, although the "phonology only" group was superior on most measures. This growth can only be linked to reading, since the researchers took careful precautions to ensure that there was no "explicit mention of phonology . . . [or] teaching strategies explicitly concerned with phonological linkage activities" (p. 48). Teachers were "frequently reminded" of this during the experiment. Correlational evidence also corroborates that phonemic awareness grows in most children as a consequence of reading and instruction, without programs to teach it. Bentin, Hammer, and Cahan (1991) found an "age" effect in the growth of phonemic awareness among their kindergarten subjects, even prior to any formal instruction in reading (though not, as they point out, unrelated to experience with print outside of school and in the home) (pp. 273–274).

Is Phonological Knowledge Really a Consequence of Reading Experience?: Some Challenges

Wagner and Stanovich, summarizing a series of five studies, claim that the relationship between free reading (reading done for pleasure) and phonological processing is "quite small" (1996, p. 214). An examination of these five studies reveals, however, that this outcome may very well be an indication that the type of phonological awareness (if any) that is needed for real reading is itself rather small. The test of free reading was similar in all of these studies, consisting of a short checklist test that has been found to be a good indicator of out-of-school reading experience. The measures of phonemic awareness and phonological processing varied, from phoneme deletion (dropping a sound from a spoken word, such as saying *trick* without the *r* sound—*tick*) to the reading of nonsense words. Two studies, Cunningham and Stanovich (1990, 1993), had no measures of reading comprehension, and another (Barker, Torgesen, & Wagner, 1992) had only a silent reading rate of connected text, not reading comprehension. Table 5.5 summarizes the correlations among free reading, reading comprehension, and phonological measures from studies cited by Wagner and Stanovich (1996), adding McBride-Chang, Mannis, Seidenberg, Custodio, and Doi (1993), which also addresses this issue.

A fairly consistent pattern exists across studies. The highest correlations are always between free reading and reading comprehension, ranging from .32 to .58, consistent with the view that more reading leads to more reading ability. The size of the relationship between free reading and the phonological task is always much smaller (range: −.04 to .35), *but so, too, is the phonological task's relationship to reading comprehension* (range: .05 to .36). Recall that our hypothesis is that more reading leads to more reading ability, and to the extent that phonemic awareness is related to reading, it will be largely a consequence of reading ability. If, however, certain measures of phonemic awareness are not strongly correlated with reading, then it follows that neither will there be a strong correlation between phonemic awareness and reading amount. This is precisely what we observe in the studies listed in Table 5.5: low to moderate correlations between phonemic awareness and reading comprehension, and similarly low to moderate correlations between phonemic awareness and free reading. The lack of a relationship, then, between phonemic awareness and reading amount is hardly troubling if phonemic awareness is not itself linked to reading ability. The failure to find a strong and consistent correlation between phonemic awareness and reading ability is problematic for Wagner and Stanovich, however, since they hold that phonological abilities are central to reading acquisition.

Other studies attempt to link print exposure directly to variations in phonological awareness. Raz and Bryant (1990) conducted a longitudinal study of the relationships among access to print, the use of rhyme, and reading comprehension among four- and five-year-olds from middle- and lower-income families. They found that none of the seven individual measures of "home environment," which included five indicators of print access, predicted scores on a rhyme detection test among their four- and five-year-old subjects. The researchers analyzed the effect of each indicator *separately*, however, which very likely underestimated the effect of print on any of their other measures. An alternative explanation for their results is that no one measure adequately taps the concept of reading experience and exposure to written language for children, and only a measure that combines the various possible sources of print experience in the home will detect its impact.

Symons, Szuszkiewicz, and Bonnell (1996) corrected this problem with a more global test of reading exposure within the household by using a measure of the

Table 5.5

Correlations of Print Exposure, Real Reading, and Phonological Tasks

STUDY	FREE READING TO PHONOLOGICAL TASK	READING COMPREHENSION TO PHONOLOGICAL TASK	FREE READING TO READING COMPREHENSION
Stanovich and West (1989)	.27 (phonological choice)	.27	.36
	.35 (pseudoword naming)	.28	
Barker, Torgesen, and Wagner (1992)	.03 (phoneme deletion)	.21	.42 (silent reading rate)
	.28 (phonological choice)	.36	
Cipielewski and Stanovich (1992)	.31 (phonetic analysis)	.31	.58
Cunningham and Stanovich (1990)	−.04 (phoneme deletion)	—	—
McBride-Chang et al. (1993) (Disabled Readers, Comparison)	.20, .26 (nonword reading)	.05, .36	.32, .64
Cunningham and Stanovich (1993)	.01, .16 (phoneme deletion) −.04 (phoneme transposition)	—	—

parent's reading experience, the assumption being that this would in turn relate to how much print exposure their children would have. Unlike Raz and Bryant (1990), Symons et al. found a significant effect for print on children's phonological awareness, even after controlling for socioeconomic variables. It appears, then, that print exposure is a sum of a number of different variables, and that analyzing each component separately may miss the cumulative effect of all sources combined—including number of books, library visits, role models in reading, and other actions associated with encounters with written language.

Vellutino and his colleagues (1996) also attempted to measure print exposure's effects on phonological awareness in their large-scale study (over 1,400 children), but here the problem was with the test itself. Vellutino et al. employed a "print conventions" measure to tap print exposure knowledge, which tests children's familiarity with written English concepts such as how books are oriented, the top-to-bottom directionality of print, the meaning of punctuation marks, and so forth. However, the "normal" readers and the three "low" groups all scored rather close to the maximum possible (12). Calculating from the standard deviation and effect sizes shown in Vellutino et al.'s Table 5, we find that the "normal" readers scored almost a perfect 12 (11.18), and the lowest of the low groups was not far behind (9.55). In other words, because all groups scored near the ceiling on this test, it is unlikely to be able to differentiate levels of print exposure among children even if variations actually existed. As we shall see in Chapter 7, when broader measures are taken, substantial differences in print exposure and access have been found to exist among children of varying reading abilities.[3]

Sound Ideas About Reading

Sound is not critical to reading, either for fluent readers or for those who are learning how to read. As Frank Smith and Ken Goodman hypothesized three decades ago, reading for meaning is not primarily a process of decoding words to sounds. While knowledge of how sound and writing relate can be helpful to some children to make sense of text when other strategies fail, the claims that have been made about the necessity of phonemic awareness and its training for early reading do not appear to be substantiated by the evidence to date. The often-noted superiority of good readers in phonemic awareness seems to be largely a product of reading experience. It is also possible to find good readers who have poor phonemic awareness, and explicit training in phonemic awareness produces relatively moderate and limited results on reading comprehension. The failure of some studies to find a strong link between print exposure and performance on phonological tasks may be due to methodological problems or perhaps even to the limited impact of those phonological abilities on real reading.

6

Context, Eye Movements, and Comparisons in Reading

Although the role of sound and phonics instruction in reading has received most of the attention in the reading debates of the past fifty years, there are other, equally important issues involved in identifying what fluent readers do and how children learn to read. I noted in the proposed model of literacy acquisition (Chapter 2) that the reception of comprehensible, written language results in reading acquisition and development. Now I return to the question of how the comprehension of text actually takes place. How is it that we are able to understand the written marks on the page? Of equal interest to us, from the practical standpoint, is the issue of whether certain approaches to helping children learn to read have been found to be more successful than others. Are methods that emphasize metalinguistic over elaborative assistance, for example, better than their alternatives? These are the issues we will take up in this chapter, beginning with a discussion of the disputed role of "context" in reading.

Making Sense of Print: The Role of Context

As your eyes scan the page, what do they see? A common perception of reading goes something like this: We examine each and every letter in sequence, assembling them all together until we have a word. From there we identify each word we encounter as we move from left to right in the text, putting these words together to form a sentence. We then gather up these sentences until we end up with a paragraph, and so forth down the page. This letter-by-letter, word-by-word approach, like the previous chapter's "sound out the word" logic, has a certain popularity, even among some researchers. But we have good reason to believe that it is not correct.

One of the oldest findings of experimental psychology is that there is a rather strict limit to the number of random letters we can identify at a single glance, usually 4 to 5 (Cattell, 1885, cited in Smith, 1973). If, however, these letters are arranged to make two or three unrelated words, we can identify perhaps a *dozen* letters or more in the form of words in the same amount of time. And if these words are themselves arranged to form a phrase or short sentence, we can in effect identify two to three dozen letters in that exact same instant, only in the form of a meaningful string of words.

How is it possible that under some conditions we can make out only four to five letters, but under other conditions identify words and phrases consisting of 20 or 30 letters? Quite simply, our prior knowledge of words and how they go together greatly facilitate the rapidity with which we can identify them. To choose among random letters means deciding among 26 alternatives at each step. By definition, there is no pattern to "speed" the process along. But as fluent readers, we know a good deal about words and how they go together, and we can eliminate in advance certain possibilities. Most of this knowledge is implicit, of course, not something we typically think about consciously. We know, for example, that the letter *q* is usually followed by the letter *u*, so that once we see a *q* we can reduce the number of possibilities for the following letter down to one. Taken to the next level, a string of meaningfully combined words (a sentence) takes less visual information to identify than would be needed to read these exact same words arranged at random. As was pointed out in Chapter 2, our nonvisual information—what we can refer to as our background knowledge or "context"—helps us identify words and meaning much faster due to the elimination of unlikely alternatives.

Trying to identify words letter by letter would be much too cumbersome for fluent reading in any case, causing an overload on what our short-term memory could handle (Smith, 1973, 1994). Instead, we typically identify words without resorting to a letter-by-letter analysis, although once identified, we can then break the word down into its constituent letters if so required. Note that this is not to say that we fail to physically *look* at the letters, or that we simply pass over the visual information contained in them. Smith (1973) noted that one of the keys to our ability to read at the speed we do is our "feature analysis" of letters and words: We "sample" from the visual information on the page, examining aspects of letters (perhaps even something from every letter) without necessarily *identifying* those letters individually as we make our determination of the entire word.[1] Similarly, we do not necessarily identify each word in succession as our eyes scan the page, but rather we identify the *meaning* conveyed by those words that make up the phrase or sentence.[2]

All this will take place in normal, fluent reading. Of course, sometimes reading "breaks down," and we fail to comprehend a phrase or word. When this happens, we may need to resort to other, less efficient strategies for making sense of print. We may stop and read more slowly, or reread, trying to identify individual words in an attempt to grasp the meaning. Under some conditions, we may even attempt to identify individual letters of words to figure them out, if the other words in the sentence do not provide their meaning for us. This is especially true if we are unnaturally forced to isolate words in a sentence, or have our attention directed at individual words, as is sometimes done in laboratory tests of reading ability. Under these confusing or contrived situations, we may make use of other ways to identify a word, such as making use of sound-letter clues.

Putting Context Studies in Context

A series of studies have been conducted over the past three decades on the role of "context" in reading, some of which are thought to contradict the Goodman-Smith view presented here (or at least as I have interpreted their view). Unfortunately, little agreement exists on what context is or how it should be defined, especially when it comes to interpreting the results of these experimental studies. As I've noted, Smith (1973, 1994) defined context broadly as primarily nonvisual background knowledge, the reader's "understanding at any given point in the text of what it is about, enhanced by what has already been seen behind and sometimes ahead of where the eye happens to fall." This knowledge of language, including syntax, semantics, sound-letter correspondences, genre, and style, "facilitates reading by reducing the reader's uncertainty" (1994, p. 275).

A somewhat narrower view of context is provided by Stanovich (1982, 1986), who defines context as what can be determined from the visual information present in the sentence or passage. Context, then, is what is "predictable" or congruous with the printed text in question. Thus, in the sentence, "The man drove his ___," the context predicts a word such as *car,* and to use context in this situation would be to say "car" if so prompted.

Like several other researchers, Stanovich further distinguishes between two "levels" of processing involved in reading: word identification and comprehension. Word identification is a "lower level" process, which involves the identification of individual words on the page. Comprehension is a "higher level" process, which is, in a sense, putting the words we've identified together to form the idea or message of the text. Context, Stanovich claims, does help "higher" level comprehension processes, but this effect has been "inappropriately generalized to the word recognition level" (Stanovich & Stanovich, 1995, p. 90) by theorists such as Smith. Stanovich concludes that word identification is *not* dependent primarily upon context, but takes place for the most part independently of it. Words are first recognized and then passed along to the "higher level" processor for comprehension. For this reason, "background knowledge and contextual information attenuate as the efficiency of word recognition processes increases" (Stanovich & Stanovich, 1995, p. 91); that is, good readers use the visual information on the page, the "context," *less* than poor readers. According to this view, we use context merely to compensate for a lack of decoding skills to identify words (Stanovich, 1986). Therefore context use—the use of the visual information on the page that shows what is predictable and congruous with the given text—is more typical of poor readers than of good ones.

Some Arguments on Context Use

Even if we accept Stanovich's definition of context, the evidence used to support his claims is not, I think, very convincing, and in many cases is ambiguous. The most common type of evidence on context use comes from studies employing a measure that we might call the "missing word" test. In this measure, the last word of the sentence is deleted and then shown to the reader after a brief pause. The reader is also shown words in a "neutral" sentence ("The next word will be ___"), where the sentence gives no clue as to the meaning of the missing word. The time it takes the reader to identify a word in the normal sentence minus the time it takes her to identify a word in the "neutral" sentence is considered to represent how much "context" facilitated the speed of reading words. Several studies using this type of test have found that the difference in how long it takes readers to identify words between the normal and neutral sentences is greater for poor readers than for good readers (e.g., Schwantes, Boesl, & Ritz, 1980; Stanovich, 1982, 1986; West & Stanovich, 1978). In other words, poor readers seem to benefit more from having words in "context" (again, in Stanovich's sense) than good readers.

There are plausible alternative explanations of these results, equally consistent with the data presented by Stanovich and his colleagues *and* with the Goodman-Smith Model, as Krashen (1998a) notes. The condition of having to identify a specific word in a sentence places the reader in an unnatural condition of focusing on identifying words rather than doing what he normally does, which is identify meaning. This shift in focus may have consequences for the strategies that will be adopted by the reader. In particular, the use of neutral-context sentences means that *all* readers will need to draw on something other than context to identify individual words. In other words, the task becomes very much like individual word identification, in which the ability to use other cues for meaning, such as sound-letter correspondences, will now be at a premium. Since better readers are *also* better than poor readers at decoding words in isolation, we should therefore expect that good readers will perform relatively faster in the neutral sentence condition compared to poor readers. The difference between the context and neutral conditions may be smaller for good readers than for poor readers because good readers can both employ their superior decoding ability in the neutral context *and* use context more effectively. This is entirely in line with the Goodman-Smith Model and the results found by Stanovich and others.

Thus, *two* variables are being tapped in the calculation of "context" in the missing word test. Stanovich (1986) was aware of this confound due to decoding ability in his context calculations and attempted to control for it by controlling for the level of decoding ability in good and poor readers via a longitudinal study. Stanovich, Cunningham, and Feeman (1984) examined a group of good and poor readers in the fall and spring of their first-grade year. The children were given two paragraphs to read: a coherent paragraph written at the first-grade level, and a "random" paragraph where those same words were listed in random order. The coherent paragraph reading was thought to measure context use, and the random list task was thought to tap decoding ability. The researchers compared the performance of the good readers in the fall with the poor readers in the spring, so that the two groups were roughly equal on the test of decoding.

Unfortunately, the way in which Stanovich and his colleagues measured context in this study rendered the results, like those of previous investigations, ambiguous on the question of poor versus good readers' use of context. Rather than use the missing word test, Stanovich et al. (1984) measured context by comparing the number of words read correctly per second on the coherent versus random paragraph. As in previous studies, they found that the poor readers seemed to benefit more from the meaningful sentence context than the good readers, since the difference between the coherent and random conditions was greater for the poor readers than the good ones. However, under the category of "words read correctly," the researchers counted only the words read by the children that appeared in the text. Unlike other studies (e.g., Goodman, 1965, 1996), any word read aloud that was not exactly the same as that found in the text, but made sense according to the context of the passage, was counted as wrong. This scoring system therefore may well have underestimated the full effects of context. Interestingly enough, the good readers actually did make more errors than the poor readers at equivalent levels of decoding ability (14.8 vs. 4.6, effect size = .8), although we don't know whether the errors were contextually appropriate or not.[3] The results from this study do not show, then, that poor readers use more context than good readers, even in the narrow sense defined by Stanovich.

Another problem underlying many of the context studies to date is that readers will not adopt strategies that will make optimal use of context when they are forced to confront a *mixture* of context and no-context sentences, as noted by Massaro and Sanocki (1993). They will, in a sense, "have their guard up" during the experimental conditions, and the "context" conditions will not truly measure what context does in normal, fluent reading. Stanovich and West (1983) attempted to answer this objection in part by "blocking" the experimental sentences used so that readers would get "mostly" context conditions (66 percent of the time) or mostly noncontext (no or incongruous) conditions (again, 66 percent of the time). But this may not solve the problem, since the occurrence of incongruous words in one-third of the sentences will alert the reader that a context strategy will not be particularly successful.

Studies in which readers are in fact allowed to use context show quite clearly that readers make heavy use of context. Sanocki and Ogden (1984) and Norris (1987) both found that when readers are placed in a situation where the experimental stimuli contain mostly congruous sentence conditions (that is, a typical reading situation), they clearly take advantage of context facilitation, even in the rather unnatural laboratory conditions of having to accurately identify or make a decision about a single word at the end of a sentence (see also Sanocki et al.,1985).[4]

Is Text Really Predictable?

Another argument used against the Goodman-Smith Model is that words are not, in fact, highly "predictable" in text, and hence context is not particularly helpful in reducing uncertainty. Citing several studies on the probability that an adult reader can predict correctly words in a text only 20 to 35 percent of the time (e.g., Finn, 1978–1979), Stanovich (1993) claims that these figures alone contradict a model of fluent reading where context plays an important role in word identification: Our "guesses" from context would be too inaccurate to be of much use. However, this same evidence can also be taken to mean that natural text contains an enormous amount of information that reduces uncertainty of upcoming words by as much as a third. More importantly, Stanovich seems to have incorrectly interpreted Smith's position on what is meant by "predictable." Smith does not claim that readers guess or accurately predict exactly what the next word of a sentence will be, only that the natural redundancy of text allows for the number of *unlikely alternatives* to be reduced. Thus, a 20 to 35 percent chance of getting the word exactly correct underestimates the true nature of the prediction. The predictability probabilities in Finn (1977–1978) are calculated based upon how well readers were able to guess the next word accurately in a given sentence during experimental conditions, not upon the amount of uncertainty reduced by context. Perfetti, Goldman, and Hogaboam (1979) report that their fifth-grade subjects (Experiment 3) gave a response to a deleted word in a passage that was either the exact word *or contextually appropriate* 58 percent of the time, demonstrating that text can provide a good deal of information in helping the reader eliminate unlikely alternatives.

A Word on Eye Movement Studies

How context is used in fluent reading has often been related to studies on how and where the eyes fixate when we read. It has been claimed that such studies demonstrate that we do not "skip" words or letters when reading, but rather, that we examine each and every unit of print available to us, contrary to what Smith is said to assert (e.g., Stanovich, 1993). The principal problem with this interpretation is that the "Skipping Hypothesis" does not appear to have been Smith's position to begin with. As noted earlier, Smith (1973, 1994) stated quite clearly that we make a "feature analysis" of letters and words as we reduce uncertainty and grasp meaning from written language, although it remains unclear precisely which features we use. "Sampling" text on the page does not require, then, that our eyes literally jump over words. Indeed, Smith conjectures that it does not seem unreasonable that we benefit from receiving a "smooth inflow of selected visual information" as we go about the business of comprehension (1994, p. 255). It is equally important to point out that we can't be said to *identify* individual letters or words one by one merely because we scan across them. Identification of individual words, if it takes place at all, may happen after the eye has already moved on to the next fixation.

There are several methodological problems in the way in which most eye fixation research is conducted, as Krashen (1998a) notes. Readers are placed in highly unnatural positions, with their heads often constricted by chin rests, bite plates, and the like. In addition, readers are instructed to pay close attention to what they are reading, since they will be tested on it when they finish, and they are forced to read rather uninteresting texts, leading to a tendency to fixate more carefully than might otherwise be the case.

Method Comparisons: Which Way Is Best?

A final point of contention in the debates over what constitutes fluent reading and how children learn to read is the subject of method comparison studies, studies that attempt to determine which approach (if any) is best in teaching children to read. It has been claimed, for example, that classroom studies show that a heavy emphasis on metalinguistic instruction produces superior results in early reading achievement, and thus investments in programs to train students in phonemic awareness and phonics will produce substantial dividends. None of the major research reviews to date, however, have been very useful in helping us answer the question of which method is best, and widely cited comparisons of teaching methods often suffer from ill-defined labels or inconclusive results.

Chall's "Great Debate" Revisited

Easily the most influential review of reading methods in the past thirty years is Jeanne Chall's *Learning To Read: The Great Debate* (1967/1983), an impressive synthesis of research on the teaching of reading. Unfortunately, Chall's 1967 review now has little methodological relevance to current debates over "whole language" versus "phonics" in early reading, yet it is still cited as "proving" that phonics and metalinguistic training is a superior approach for teaching reading. Chall compared what she called "meaning-emphasis" versus "code-emphasis" methods, but many of the "meaning-emphasis" methods examined often had little in common with our current understanding of how children make sense of texts as outlined in Chapters 2 and 3. One "meaning-emphasis" method in particular, "Look-Say" or "whole word," was defined by what it *wasn't*—teaching children explicitly about letter-sound correspondences ("phonics"). This meant that even rather meaningless activities, such as the Look-Say strategy of memorizing "sight words" in isolation, were counted as "meaning-emphasis" as long as there was no explicit phonics teaching. The other "meaning-emphasis" method in Chall's book, "intrinsic phonics," was said to combine some teaching of letter-sound correspondences in the context of other (equally undefined) instruction. The "code-emphasis" approach analyzed in the book was "systematic phonics," where children were taught about sounds and letters in a systematic way not necessarily related to what they were trying to read, or often before they were exposed to real reading at all.

The uncertainty about what actually went on in the classrooms compared in Chall's review should be reason enough for casting doubt on any conclusions drawn from it. In particular, it must be stressed again that the "meaning-emphasis" approaches in Chall bear little or no relation to current materials and methods of teaching reading, so citation of Chall's reviews does nothing to bolster the case for present-day advocates of metalinguistic instruction. What is perhaps more interesting (and surprising, given the influence of the first edition of her book) is the weakness of Chall's original evidence in favor of explicit, direct, and systematic phonics instruction, even compared to the ill-defined "Look-Say" and "intrinsic phonics" methods. The results summarized in Chapter 4 of her book reveal that deciding on a superior method based on the studies she reviews amounts to little more than a coin toss. Table 6.1 summarizes a "vote count" of the silent and oral reading comprehension measures used in Grades One and Two.[5]

No method is clearly favored in the first and second grades when it comes to reading comprehension, and none of the studies Chall reviewed that included phonics/no phonics comparisons extended beyond the second grade. In a separate

Table 6.1

Vote Count of Findings from Grades 1 and 2 Studies Reviewed by Chall (1967)

	STUDIES FAVORING
No Phonics ("Look-Say")	4
Some Phonics	2
Intensive, Systematic Phonics	4
No Difference	1

(from Chall, 1967/1983, Tables 4-1A & 4-1B)

comparison (Chall's Table 4-2B), the differences between "intrinsic" versus "systematic" phonics were found to be neglible on silent and oral reading measures. The systematic phonics was superior in 8 findings, the smaller dosage of phonics (intrinsic) was better in 4 cases, and no difference was found in another 4 studies. Superior results in only half of the studies is not particularly strong evidence for a pro-phonics position.

Reviews of "Whole Language"

More recent attempts to summarize the research literature on method comparisons have been equally difficult to interpret, largely for the same reasons that plague Chall's review: vague labels, poor study quality, and limited information about what actually went on in the classes studied. Stahl and Miller (1989) compared a combination of "whole language" (WL) and "language experience approach" (LEA) studies to methods that focused more on teaching "skills" and using skill-based "basal" reading materials. As in the case of Chall's "Look-Say," however, the categories used in the Stahl and Murray review, whole language and language experience approach, in reality covered a multitude of methods. It is not clear what exactly was being compared in many studies, or even whether WL and LEA can be combined under a single heading (McGee & Lomax, 1990; Schickedanz, 1990).

The language experience approach involves, in essence, having children dictate stories to the teacher and read the product, although other elements are included in some programs. "Whole language" was defined in Stahl and Miller's (1989) review as having the following characteristics: (1) There is an emphasis on using children's own language, (2) the class is "child-centered" rather than "teacher-centered," (3) the use of real story books is promoted over commercial basal readers, and (4) phonics is only taught in the context of meaningful reading, if at all. It should be noted that a great deal could go on under these descriptors, none of which specifies that children will necessarily have more contact with comprehensible print. Unfortunately, Stahl and Miller found that, even if specific program descriptions were included, "few studies used observations to verify fidelity to the intended method" (p. 92). Given the heterogeneity of the studies used for both comparison groups, it is not surprising

Table 6.2

Amount Spent on Various Reading Activities in Basal and LEA Classrooms
(in Minutes/Day) and Relationship to Reading Achievement

READING ACTIVITY	BASAL CLASSROOMS	LANGUAGE EXPERIENCE APPROACH CLASSROOMS	CORRELATION WITH READING COMPREHENSION
Reading Basal	48.1 (13.1)	5.9 (8.1)	.47*
LEA Chart Stories	11.3 (8.0)	24.9 (5.9)	−.13
Sight Word Teaching	14.3 (6.5)	15.5 (5.9)	.24
Phonics	14.6 (4.7)	14.8 (3.4)	.16
Drawing Pictures with Stories	8.4 (6.1)	18.6 (7.4)	−.31*
"Other" Reading Activities	7.4 (5.7)	22.5 (12.3)	−.09

(from Harris & Serwer, 1966, Tables 5 and 6.)
* = statistically significant, alpha = .05

that Stahl and Miller found the overall differences between WL/LEA and basal/skill approaches to be virtually nonexistent (effect size = .09, favoring whole language/ language experience approach).

Some of the studies included in Stahl and Miller's review illustrate that the label placed on a program is less important than what actually takes place in the classroom. This is particularly true of some of the LEA studies or of those investigations where it was not clear in the description how much actual real reading students did. Harris and Serwer (1966)—one of a series of United States Department of Education–sponsored early reading studies included in both Stahl and Miller's (1989) review as well as in the second edition of Chall's (1967/1983) book—discovered that the children in basal/ skills groups actually did *more* reading than the LEA classes they studied. Table 6.2 shows the amount of time spent by teachers in basal/skills and LEA classrooms and the standard deviations, an indication of variability within a given method.

Note that two groups did about the same amount of phonics instruction (about 15 minutes), but the basal group spent nearly *twice* as much time actually reading either a commercial basal or LEA chart stories, 59.4 minutes versus 30.8 for the LEA group. For all teachers combined, the amount of time spent on the basal reader was positively correlated to reading comprehension (r = .47). This does not mean, of course, that we should return to the often stilted "Dick-and-Jane"-style basal readers. Interesting and well-written story books can also be read by children. It may mean, however, that providing lots of opportunities to read comprehensible texts may be a more important criterion for comparing classroom instruction than "basal" or "LEA" designations.

Since Stahl and Miller (1989) note that few of their studies took such careful approaches to measuring how programs were actually implemented, it is difficult to

Table 6.3

Percentage of Time Spent on Reading Activities in LEA and Traditional Classrooms
(Teacher-Led Group)

ACTIVITIES	TRADITIONAL	LEA	CORRELATION WITH READING COMPREHENSION
Sight Word Practice	5.33 (3.15)	8.37 (9.32)	−.04
Word Analysis	13.38 (6.69)	5.37 (1.84)	.14
Oral Reading of Text	4.32 (2.59)	7.42 (8.38)	.09
Silent Reading of Text	6.72 (4.69)	6.91 (8.39)	.53

(from Evans & Carr, 1985, Tables 1 and 6) Percentage of time is out of one-half day of instruction.

make generalizations on how inaccurate labeling in other studies may have affected their results. An analysis of instructional time by Evans and Carr (1985), another study included in the Stahl and Miller review, is not encouraging on this point, however. Like Harris and Serwer (1966), Evans and Carr found that "language-oriented" LEA groups differed from "routinized performance" traditional classrooms in time spent on some activities but not others, and not always in the expected direction. Table 6.3 displays some of these differences.

The most important thing to note in Table 6.3 is that the LEA group did *not* spend considerably more time on reading than the traditionally taught classes, particularly on teacher-led silent reading, which had the largest single correlation with the reading comprehension test (.53). The traditional group spent considerably more time on phonics activities (word analysis), and the LEA more on sight-words practice.

Stahl and his colleagues (Stahl, McKenna, & Pagnucco, 1994) reviewed studies that were published after the Stahl and Miller (1989) metaanalysis and reported that whole language approaches did better in four studies, skills in one study, and no difference was found in 12 others. However, it is unclear from their report which studies were classified under which category. In addition, since many of the included studies were unpublished, it is very difficult to determine whether "whole language" really meant more reading than the traditionally taught groups. We are thus left with the same problems of imprecise labels that plague previous reviews.

When "Whole Language" Means Real Reading

It does little good to attempt to judge the adequacy of teaching techniques merely by various labels that are attached to them, as the evidence above suggests. In fact, it is probably best to avoid such labels altogether, in that they are open to interpretation, and focus instead on the actual description of events in the classroom. Instead, we need to examine studies in which an approach, however labeled ("whole language," "literature-based"), is clearly defined and/or includes measures of activities where

Table 6.4

Reading Comprehension Results for Literature-Based and Control Classrooms

MEASURE	EXPERIMENTAL 1	EXPERIMENTAL 2	CONTROL
Probed Recall[a]	23.13	21.22	14.59
CTBS Reading Comprehension[a]	62.62	62.61	59.54

[a] = posttest means adjusted for pretest scores
(from Morrow, 1992, Tables 3 and 9)

students are exposed to more meaningful print as compared to classrooms where less exposure is given or those where the focus is more on isolated skills. When this is done, we see that approaches heavy in print exposure are almost always superior (and no worse) than the alternatives. Some of these studies examine results in terms of reading achievement, while others look at reading attitudes, habits, or related behaviors (e.g., amount and quality of writing).

Reading Comprehension

Several recent studies have found "print-rich" classrooms to produce superior results in reading comprehension when compared to more skills-oriented approaches. Morrow (1992) undertook a large sample study (n = 166) in nine second-grade classrooms located in ethnically and socioeconomically diverse schools. A clear difference in the amount the experimental and control groups read and were read to is indicated in the treatment descriptions provided. The two experimental groups both received heavy doses of print exposure via access to a well-stocked classroom library and teacher-guided reading activities that emphasized reading to children, independent reading of books, and making and reading student-created books. In addition, one experimental group participated in a "home-based" reading program, where parents were encouraged to read to their children and engage them in reading. The control group used the traditional basal reader program, along with some reading aloud to the children. Table 6.4 lists measures used by Morrow that relate specifically to reading comprehension.

The experimental groups that received greater exposure to print had superior comprehension in the probed recall measure, which tapped both traditional comprehension elements (detail, cause and effect, inference) as well as story structure (plot, setting, theme). No difference was found on the comprehension subtest of the Comprehensive Test of Basic Skills (CTBS).[6]

A large-scale study conducted by Knapp and associates (1995) examined school performance over a two-year period in a variety of areas in over 140 grade one through six classrooms in schools located in low-income communities. The researchers classified their classrooms as having high, medium, and low "meaning emphasis"

Table 6.5
Meaning Emphasis in 66 Classrooms

	HIGH-MEANING	MODERATE-MEANING	LOW-MEANING
Minutes/Day Reading	48	18	5
Read/Write Integration (%)	68	36	10
Discuss Reading (%)	69	37	12
Deeper Understanding (%)	33	20	18
Skills in Context (1-3 scale)	2.3	1.8	1.6

(from Knapp et al., 1995, Figure 4-1)

in reading. A "meaning emphasis" included spending time on reading texts, discussing texts, focusing on "deeper understanding," integrating reading and writing, and teaching skills within the context of reading rather than in isolation (pp. 66–67). Results from 66 of the 140 classrooms in the first year of the study revealed some dramatic differences in emphasis, as noted in Table 6.5. Students in the "high-meaning" classrooms spent nearly ten times as many minutes reading as the "low-meaning" classes, and devoted a substantially greater percentage of their day to talking about their reading, connecting reading and writing activities, and engaging in more thoughtful discussion of texts.

The results in terms of reading comprehension (CTBS test) among all 140 classrooms were analyzed first by comparing those students in only the high- and low-meaning groups (about a third in each category). Table 6.6 summarizes the results, reported in terms of Normal Curve Equivalent (NCE) scores. Note these are not simple gain scores, but posttest score differences adjusted for initial pretest performance and the students' poverty level. The number of students tested in the nine-month cycle was much greater (more than a thousand) versus the twelve-month measures (around 450).

Meaning-emphasis classrooms did significantly better in year one (grades 1, 3, and 5), and better (but not significantly so) in year two (grades 2, 4, and 6) when measured over a single academic year. The twelve-month gains were less impressive, with no significant differences reported in the smaller sample of students used. Still, it is important to keep in mind the unusually large number of schools, classrooms, and students compared in Knapp et al.'s analysis, such that the generally positive direction of the results is still quite impressive.

Freppon (1991) investigated the abilities of 24 first graders randomly selected from two skills-based and two literature-based classrooms. While the study is only quasi-experimental in design in that Freppon examined existing classrooms, her results are indicative of the impact that immersion in meaningful written language can have. Observations were made in each classroom to measure the amount and type of interactions that took place, and her data indicate that the literature-based class-

Table 6.6

NCE Reading Score Differences of High- and Low-Meaning Emphasis Classrooms

	9 MONTHS (FALL TO SPRING)	12 MONTHS (FALL TO FALL)
Grades 1, 3, & 5 (Year 1)	+5.6	−0.5
Grades 2, 4, & 6 (Year 2)	+1.4	+3.3

+ = favors meaning emphasis
(from Knapp et al., 1995, Figures 7.1 & 7.2)

rooms did indeed engage children in more meaningful print in terms of the amount of time spent reading (18–20 minutes versus 5–9 minutes in the skills classrooms) and reading to the children (6–10 minutes versus none). Freppon measured the children's ability to comprehend passages via an "altered passage" test, where children were asked if a certain passage made sense and if not, why not, as well as an oral reading measure. The literature-based students rejected the nonsensical passages at significantly higher rates than the students in the skills classroom and were much more likely to comment on how it was not storylike or didn't make sense. The two groups were equally accurate in their oral reading. Ironically, the literature-based students were much more successful in actually sounding out words correctly in the stories as compared to the children in the skills group (53 percent to 35 percent), although the latter had received more instruction of sound-letter correspondences.

Positive results have been found in other studies where students clearly engaged in more reading and had greater access to print than comparison skills groups. Hagerty, Hiebert, and Owens (1989) studied children across three grades (2, 4, and 6) in 12 literature- and skills-based classrooms. Students in the literature-based classes outperformed those in the skills classes on the reading comprehension portion of the standardized test, controlling for pretest differences. Eldredge (1991) similarly found that a "modified whole language" approach produced better reading comprehension results than a traditional basal method for 56 first-grade students from schools serving low socioeconomic communities. Klesius, Griffith, and Zielonka (1991) did not find significant differences in reading comprehension between their "whole language" and traditionally taught first-grade classrooms. It is clear, though, that the teachers involved were slow to implement the changes in the curriculum, and the likely result was that the children in the whole language classrooms did not in fact experience a significantly greater amount of exposure to text.

Reading Attitudes and Habits

As in the case of reading comprehension, students in classrooms with a print-exposure focus have been found to be superior in terms of their attitudes toward reading and the amount of reading they do. These factors should not be taken lightly:

It does little good to teach children to read if, when they leave school, they hate reading. Morrow's (1992) study discussed above also included a measure of the amount of reading done by the participating students. She found that the literature-based classes not only read better than the control groups, but also reported reading more books and magazines. The children were also able to name more books and authors, confirming the fact that they had more exposure to print. Eldredge (1991) also found that his modified whole language groups had significantly more positive attitudes toward reading as a result of their exposure to more reading. The researcher-created attitude measure had 100 items; whole language students averaged 79.54 (standard deviation = 19.3), the basal students, 71.59 (standard deviation = 20.3).

McKenna, Stratton, Grindler, and Jenkins (1995) conducted three studies on the effect of different approaches to early reading instruction on reading attitudes. The first two studies found no differences between students in schools said to be engaging in "whole language" and traditional instruction, but no actual teacher practices were measured or observed. A third study did look at the impact of individual "whole language" teachers on reading attitude more closely, this time focusing on the specific environment of successful and less successful teachers in terms of producing positive reading attitudes among students. Here clear differences were noted: The more successful teachers in terms of promoting higher reading motivation among students had more print on display and books accessible for students.

Gambrell (1996) reports on a large-scale 10-week project, "Running Start," to increase reading motivation among elementary school students. Classrooms were provided with approximately 50 to 60 new books, and additional home and school reading was encouraged. One study with 550 first-grade students found that the print-access program was indeed more successful in increasing students' motivation to read than traditional approaches. Students in the Running Start program were more motivated, took more books home to read, and spent more time reading. These positive effects appeared to be long-lasting: A selection of students who participated in the project were interviewed six months later, and the significant differences among students in motivation and reading habits persisted.[7] Finally, Mervar and Hiebert (1989) studied the amount that students actually read at school and home in two different instructional approaches for 20 second-grade children. The students in literature-based classrooms spent considerably more time choosing books in the school library (mean of 11.6 minutes versus 2.60 for the skills group) and were much more sophisticated in the way they chose their books (e.g., sampling the text, inspecting more than one book, using the card catalog).

Other Literacy Measures

Several of the studies cited above also included other measures of literacy performance in comparing types of reading instruction. Morrow (1992) included several measures of the written work by children in her literature-based and traditional basal classrooms and found that the children in the experimental groups did significantly better in several measures, including story structure, variety of vocabulary, and quantity of writing. Children in Morrow's literature-based classes were also superior in the ability to retell stories in oral and written form.

Similarly, Purcell-Gates, McIntyre, and Freppon (1995) found that students in kindergarten and first-grade classrooms where greater emphasis was placed on reading to children and with children made greater gains in their use of literate language than those in skills-emphasis classes. Large amounts of time were devoted to read-alouds and giving children time to read self-selected books, while the skills groups spent considerably less time engaged in reading. The results of children's written language samples revealed significant differences in the frequency and breadth of literate language. Hagerty et al. (1989), who noted a significant advantage for literature-based classrooms in reading comprehension (described above), found no differences on writing scores across the three grade levels they studied.

A small-scale study by Freppon (1995) found that a group of students (N = 17) who had attended whole language kindergarten and first-grade classrooms began to change their perceptions of reading when they attended a more skills-oriented class in grade two. No differences were found in a test of oral-reading accuracy, but other differences emerged between those who continued receiving whole language instruction and those who did not. Children from the skills-oriented classes showed much less knowledge about things to read outside of class than the literature-based classes, wrote less in their journals, and produced less literate language in their writing.

An Exception to the Rule?: The Foorman Study

Studies in which children are clearly exposed to more text typically do better (and never worse) than those in classrooms with less focus on print exposure or ones in which skills or phonics receive heavy emphasis. Despite the consistency of these findings, one widely publicized study has recently been reported to show that a heavier use of metalinguistic instruction produced better results than the alternative approaches. While the final version of the study has not yet been published, a preliminary version was made available by the principal investigator in the study, Barbara Foorman (Foorman, Francis, Beeler, Winikates, & Fletcher, in press). Unfortunately, no strong conclusions can be drawn about the data as they appear in this version of the study. Missing is detailed information on *what actually took place* in the "whole language" and "phonics" treatments for the children involved; that is, it is not clear whether the "whole language" group actually had more exposure to print than the "phonics" group. Preliminary results found no differences between the two groups on a combined reading-comprehension and word-identification test, and both groups scored very low on a Formal Reading Inventory comprehension assessment.

Conclusion: No Phonics?

Previous reviews of reading instruction methods have used vague labels to define approaches, attempted to equate approaches that differ in significant ways, and generally failed to define very carefully the amount of actual print exposure children receive in class. All of these problems leave open to question the conclusions of these efforts. When we restrict ourselves to (an admittedly) much smaller group of studies in which the differences between groups in terms of the amount of connected reading of text is more clearly established, then students overall do better in a variety of literacy measures. I should stress again that this does not mean that some metalinguistic instruction, for some children, may not be useful, which is consistent with our discussion in previous chapters. However, the notion that an emphasis primarily on skills and phonics instruction produces superior results to programs centered on providing children with a lot of interesting and comprehensible texts is not supported by the available evidence.

7

Real Crises, Real Solutions

The Limits of Method

After having taught in, observed in, and written about schools for more than a decade, John Holt made the following observation more than twenty-five years ago:

> Many . . . people are demanding better reading programs in their schools. They might be wiser to try to get more branch libraries in their districts, or better yet, neighborhood storefront libraries or traveling bookmobiles, with newspapers, periodicals, and paperbacks—the kinds of reading material we know kids like to read. What's the point of having kids learn to read if after they've learned there's nothing *to* read . . . *Access to reading matter, not reading methods, is the name of the game.* (Holt, 1972/1993, pp. 205–206; emphasis added)

Warwick Elley, director of the International Association for the Evaluation of Educational Achievements' (IEA) 1992 international study of reading in 32 countries involving more than 200,000 students, came to this conclusion in 1994, after having examined the results of that massive undertaking:

> *Acceptable levels of literacy are achieved by most pupils, in most systems, despite a diversity of reading methods and traditions.* In general, however, achievement is greatest when the educational systems are well endowed financially, when teachers are well educated, when students have ready access to good books, when they enjoy reading and do it often, and when their first language is the same as that of the language of the school. (Elley, 1994, pp. xxi–xxii; emphasis added)

The similarity of these conclusions, one reached after years of careful observation, the other the product of sophisticated statistical calculation, is striking. The availability of books to read—and the subsequent amount of reading done—appears to be as critical, and certainly no less so, in determining success in reading as classroom instructional methods. This is *not* to say that teaching methods are unimportant, nor that access to

Table 7.1
Correlations Between Reading Method and State NAEP Score

PERCENTAGE OF TEACHERS USING:	CORRELATION WITH NAEP SCORE	CONTROLLED FOR POVERTY
Whole Language	.07	.006
Phonics	−.59	−.07

(from NCES, 1994)

print is the exclusive or sufficient condition for literacy. We have seen that different methods can have very distinct outcomes, and individual children may need different types of assistance. But without access to print, teaching methodology can have only a limited impact and may not, in any case, be capable of explaining significant variations in reading achievement observed between school districts, states, and countries.

An illustration of this point comes from the National Assessment of Educational Progress (NAEP) scores, the reading test given to a nationally representative sample of United States schoolchildren every two years. Table 7.1 shows the correlations between the NAEP scores and the percentage of teachers in a state who say they used "whole language" teaching and those who favored "phonics" approaches. Data are drawn from the 1992 fourth-grade scores (National Center for Education Statistics, 1994). The second column in Table 7.1 shows the simple correlation between reported reading method and a state's NAEP score. For whole language, the figure is a nonsignificant .07, close to zero. For phonics, it is negative and significant, at −.59. However, it is also true that phonics is used more heavily in poor states than in wealthy ones, so that to distinguish the possibly negative effects of poverty in general and phonics use in particular, it is necessary to control for poverty (here represented by a composite of the percentage of children in a state living in poverty [Bureau of the Census, 1995] and the percentage of schools in the state with more than 75 percent of their students enrolled in free lunch programs). As can be seen in the table, the "whole language" correlation becomes even closer to zero, and the phonics relationship is similarly nonsignificant and miniscule at −.07.

Unfortunately, these "self-reports" of teaching method are not always accurate, and the labels "whole language" and "phonics" may simply be too vague to be of much use. But the NAEP data is the best we have on classroom practices in United States classrooms, and the failure to find any relationship between method and achievement suggests that, from a policy standpoint, we may not wish to limit our focus to teaching method as the sole or primary factor in explaining why reading scores differ from one place to another, particularly when it comes to large-scale differences as have been observed among schools and states. It is conceivable that the variations in the supply of reading materials may overwhelm differences in teaching methods, given that teachers and students are limited by the resources available to them. Let us now examine the effect that variations in access have in predicting reading success and failure.

Figure 7.1
The Relationship between Print Access and Reading

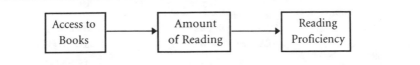

Evidence on the Importance of Access

In our model of literacy acquisition outlined in Chapter 2, it was suggested that literacy development is dependent on the amount of reading done which, in turn, is affected by the amount of reading material available to the reader (Krashen, 1993). This relationship is shown in Figure 7.1.

Reading instruction can intervene in the model, of course, by making reading more comprehensible in a variety of ways and thus increasing the amount of reading done. I begin with the evidence for the second part of the model, more reading means better reading, since it is fairly well agreed upon among researchers along all points of the methodological spectrum.

More Reading Leads to Better Reading Achievement

A variety of investigations of the relationship between the amount of reading and reading performance have been done, from simple surveys to experimental studies. The most recent NAEP test results provide a straightforward illustration of the connection between reading frequency and achievement, as shown in Table 7.2: Students who read more, read better.

More sophisticated research methods have found similar results. Anderson et al. (1988) had fifth-grade students keep a diary of all of their out-of-school activities over a period of several weeks. Table 7.3 shows the percentile rank on a standardized achievement test, the amount of reading in minutes (including books, comics, newspapers, and magazines), and the estimated number of words read per year. Note that the more reading students did, the higher their reading score.

The range of time and amount of reading is quite stunning: from 1.5 hours to less than 2 minutes per day, and from close to 5,000,000 words to around 50,000 words read per year. Not surprisingly, Anderson and his colleagues found that the

Table 7.2
Fourth Graders' Self-Reported Reading Frequency and 1994 NAEP Score

ALMOST EVERY DAY	1–2 TIMES A WEEK	NEVER/HARDLY EVER
221	217	198

(from NCES, 1994)

Table 7.3
Amount of Time Spent Reading and Reading Achievement
of Fifth Graders (N = 155)

PERCENTILE RANK	MINUTES OF TEXT READING PER DAY	ESTIMATED NUMBER OF WORDS READ PER YEAR
98	90.7	4,733,000
90	40.4	2,357,000
70	21.7	1,168,000
50	12.9	601,000
20	3.1	134,000
10	1.6	51,000

(from Anderson et al.,1988; Table 3)

amount of time spent reading was the best predictor of reading achievement. To test whether the amount of outside reading was really responsible for reading growth over the period of the study, Anderson and his colleagues controlled for the effects of the students' previous test scores (from grade two). The result was a positive correlation between reading achievement for book reading (.29) and comic book reading (.19). Taylor ét al. (1990) similarly found in their study using reading logs to measure time spent reading that the amount of silent reading done in school was a significant predictor of growth in reading comprehension among fifth and sixth graders, after having controlled for previous reading ability.

An alternative to reading logs for measuring the amount of reading done was developed using signal-detection "recognition checklists," where subjects indicate whether or not they recognize a certain author or title. Real choices are mixed in with false selections to correct for guessing. The idea is that those who recognize more authors or titles have, in fact, read more (West, Stanovich, & Mitchell, 1993). Moderate to strong positive correlations between these measures of print exposure and literacy indicators have been found at all age levels, and across languages. A summary of the results of a selection of these studies is shown in Table 7.4. Those who read more have better reading comprehension, better vocabulary, and better writing skills. These relationships, while expressed in simple correlation form in Table 7.4, have been found to survive multiple regression analysis when several other related variables are entered into the equation, including other forms of school achievement.

The correlational relationship between amount of reading and reading achievement has been confirmed in a large body of experimental research. Krashen (1993) reviewed 41 studies on "sustained silent reading" (SSR) programs, where students are given a certain amount of time each day (usually 10–20 minutes) to read a book for pleasure. These students typically do as well as or better than those who engage in traditional classroom instruction. When given a long enough opportunity to

Table 7.4
Recognition Checklist Studies: Print Exposure and Literacy Development

STUDY	LANGUAGE/AGE	PRINT EXPOSURE MEASURE	LITERACY MEASURE & CORRELATION	
Cipielewski and Stanovich (1992)	English/3rd and 5th graders	Book Titles	Read. Comp.:	.49 .58
Stanovich and Cunningham (1992)	English/college	Author Names Magazine Titles	Read. Comp.:	.54 .48
McBride-Chang et al. (1993)	English/5th–9th graders	Book Titles	Read. Comp.: .64, .32*	
West et al. (1993)	English/adults	Author Names Magazine Titles	Vocabulary:	.62 .48
Stanovich and Cunningham (1993)	English/college	Author Names Newspaper Titles	Read. Comp.:	.44 .34
Stanovich, West, and Harrison (1995)	English/college & older adults (>66 years old)	Author Names Magazine Titles	Vocabulary: .63, .60 .51, .41**	
Lee, Krashen, and Tse (1997)	English/adults	Author Names	Vocabulary:	.55
Rodrigo, McQuillan, and Krashen (1996)	Spanish/adults	Author Names	Vocabulary:	.75
Lee and Krashen (1996)	Chinese/high schoolers	Author Names	Writing:	.22

* = .62 is for what McBride-Chang et al. classified as "nondisabled" readers, .32 for "disabled" readers
** = First correlation is for older adults, second for college students

operate, SSR programs almost always show superior results to programs with less exposure to print. These impressive experimental results are true for second-language learners as well. In the United States, programs designed for "heritage language" speakers, those who come from families where a language other than English is spoken, have shown that more reading leads to more literacy development at a variety of age levels (McQuillan, in press: c). Similar results have been found in a number of large-scale experimental studies involving more than 10,000 elementary and middle school students studying English as a foreign language in several different countries and across a number of first languages. Children supplied with comprehensible texts outperform those with less reading exposure in all categories of language proficiency, including reading comprehension, writing, grammatical accuracy, and even listening comprehension (Elley, 1991, 1997).[1]

More Access Leads to More Reading

The connection between the amount of reading done and reading proficiency has been well known and accepted for a number of years. Less well known but of equal importance has been the finding that more access to reading materials *leads to* more reading, and subsequently higher reading achievement, and can itself explain a great deal of variation in reading scores. As noted in the previous chapter, Morrow (1992) found that increasing the access to books for second-grade classes in classroom literacy centers (libraries) and teacher-guided literature activities led to more reading by the experimental groups and higher levels of reading achievement by the end of her study. Table 7.5 compares the pre- and posttest survey responses of students who had increased library access and those who did not. Note that while the experimental groups increased their amount of reading dramatically over the course of the treatment, the control group saw only minimal changes.

Halle, Kurtz-Costes, and Mahoney (1997) also found that print access had a powerful effect on reading achievement. The researchers examined parental attitudes and behaviors among a group of African American families (n = 41 children) with third- and fourth-grade children attending an inner-city school. Halle and her colleagues took a number of different behavioral and attitudinal measures before the school year began and correlated them with reading achievement scores 9 months later. Interestingly, the parental "instruction" variables, such as the frequency with which parents spoke to their children about certain topics, told their children how to pronounce words correctly, taught them the names of countries and states, and so forth, were not correlated with test scores. The *only* behavior measure on the part of parents that correlated significantly with reading scores was the number of books in the home. This was true even after controlling for the level of the mother's education and their reading scores a year earlier. This is, as the researchers point out, a rather conservative estimate of the effects of book access, since the reading level of the children of the previous year is highly correlated to current reading achievement,

Table 7.5
The Effects of Increased Print Access on Reading Habits

Activity	EXPERIMENTAL 1		EXPERIMENTAL 2		CONTROL	
	Pre	*Post*	*Pre*	*Post*	*Pre*	*Post*
Read a book	12.6	18.4	13.6	20.5	12.1	13.6
Read a magazine	2.8	14.2	3.6	16.2	3.2	5.6

(from Morrow, 1992)

and the mother's level of education and number of books in the home are also positively correlated. The correlation found, then, between books at home and reading scores ($r = .29$) would almost certainly be much stronger had these controls not been in place, making their findings all the more striking.

Not surprisingly, Halle and colleagues (1997) concluded that providing reading materials to low-income African American students may be one of the most important things schools can do. They point out that while providing books in the home may appear to be within the parents' control, it is in fact "limited by the amount of time, money [and] skills available to provide these supportive resources" (p. 534), and that "within a community that has severely limited financial resources . . . the responsibility for creating a literacy-enhanced environment need not be shouldered entirely by individual families . . . *Because many of these families cannot afford to purchase children's books, it becomes all the more important to make community resources . . . easily and readily available within disadvantaged communities*" (p. 535, emphasis added).

Similar results connecting print access to more reading have been obtained at the elementary and junior high school levels in other studies. In an innovative experiment, Dorrell and Carroll (1981) put noncirculating comic books in the library, then measured the average daily circulation of *non*comic materials. The results were remarkable: Circulation due to increased use of the library jumped 30 percent, demonstrating that merely increasing access to books increases the likelihood that they will be read. Ramos and Krashen (in press) report an equally dramatic result with elementary school students who previously had little access to books. After they were taken to the local public library, the amount of reading and enthusiasm for reading increased dramatically among students. Rucker (1982) reports that a random sample of junior high school students who were given two free subscriptions to magazines related to their interests for one year scored significantly higher on standardized tests of reading compared to a control group. Neither the students nor the teachers knew of the experiment, but the power of print access was substantial all the same.

The relationship between access to reading matter and reading frequency is also demonstrated in a set of case studies by Worthy (1996), who looked at eleven "reluctant" readers in middle school, where she conducted observations of and interviews with each student. Worthy found that the primary reasons for students' infrequent reading was not that they dislike reading *per se* "but because [they do] not have access at home to the kinds of reading materials that interest [them]" (p. 485). Access was one of three barriers to reading Worthy identified among her informants (the other two were a lack of choice in the books assigned to them and the absence of opportunities in school to read for pleasure). The students noted that they had little access at home to the kinds of reading materials they enjoyed, and the school library was unable to fill that gap.

Larger-scale correlational studies provide supporting evidence of the positive effects of print access on reading frequency and achievement. Lance, Wellborn, and Hamilton-Pennell (1993) found at the state level that the access to books in school via the library was the most powerful predictor of academic achievement among several variables analyzed, controlling for socioeconomic status. (At two of the six grade levels that Lance et al. analyzed, school library quality was actually a *more* powerful predictor of reading scores than socioeconommic status measures.) Krashen (1995) found a similar relationship for elementary school students when examining data at the national level in the United States. Controlling for per pupil spending per state and computer software holdings, Krashen found that the quality of the school library was a significant predictor of fourth-grade NAEP reading scores.

International comparisons show the same strong effects of print access on reading achievement. Elley's (1994, 1996) comparison of reading score, home environment, and school and public library data from several countries came to the conclusion that *access to print was the most powerful correlate of reading achievement*. Controlling for differences in economic conditions among the participating countries, Elley (1996) found that the size of the school library was the number one factor distinguishing the reading scores of nine-year-olds between the high and low scoring nations, with an impressive effect size of .82. Frequent silent reading time was the next most important variable, with an effect size of .78.

Print Access, Free Reading, and NAEP Reading Scores: Ranking the States

My own analysis of the 1992 state NAEP reading scores provides yet another indicator of how important print access is in determining reading achievement. By measuring the amount of print access and the frequency of reading by state, we can see how state rankings compare to their performance on reading.[2] Table 7.6 shows a list of variables drawn from the NAEP surveys and other federal sources on school and home resources related to print access and reading achievement. Print access was here defined as that consisting of the three likely sources of reading matter for children: the home, the school library, and the public library (McQuillan, 1997a). In addition, a measure of the amount of reading and level of poverty present in a state were also included. Table 7.7 shows the rankings of the states in Free Reading, Total Print Access (home, school, and community), and NAEP reading scores.

An inspection of the scores in Table 7.7 will reveal the strong relationship between how much print access a state has, how frequently students read, and reading achievement. We note in Table 7.8 that more print access is correlated positively with free reading ($r = .720$), suggestive that the better access children in a state have to reading materials at home, in school, and in the community, the more they read. Print access and free reading are also closely related to test scores: reading proficiency correlates .852 with Total Print Access, and .644 with Free Reading. This means that simply knowing how much print access students have in a state can explain 73 percent of the variance in reading test scores; knowing how much free reading takes place accounts for 41 percent of the variance.

One possible criticism of this analysis is that print access is merely a proxy for larger socioeconomic influences on reading achievement. When we calculate the correlation between poverty (defined in Table 7.6) and a state's NAEP score, the relationship is indeed as strong as the one between print access and reading achievement, in the opposite direction ($r = -.77$). However, even after we control for the effects of poverty statistically, we see that the effects of print access on reading scores remains

Table 7.6
List of Variables Used in Analysis

Poverty

1. School Lunch: The percentage of schools in the state with more than 75 percent of their students enrolled in free lunch programs.

2. Children in Poverty: The percentage of children five- to seventeen-years-old in the state who live in families with income below the federal poverty line (Bureau of the Census, 1995).

Total Print Access

Home

3. Books at Home: The percentage of families having more than 25 books in the home.

4. Magazines: The percentage of families subscribing to at least 1 magazine regularly.

5. Newspaper: The percentage of families subscribing to 1 newspaper.

School

6. School Library Books: The number of books per pupil in the school library (White, 1990).

7. School Library Subscriptions: The number of magazine subscriptions per pupil in the school library (White, 1990).

Community

8. Public Library Books: The number of books per person in the public library (NCES, 1995).

9. Public Library Subscriptions: The number of magazine subscriptions per person in the public library (NCES, 1995).

Free Reading

10. Books Read: The percentage of students who read at least 1 book for their own enjoyment in the last month.

11. Frequency: The percentage of students who read for fun on their own time at least once a month.

12. Sustained Silent Reading (SSR): The percentage of students who are provided time for reading books of their own choosing in school at least once a week (as reported by the student).

Reading Comprehension

13. NAEP Score: The average state NAEP fourth-grade reading score.

Note: All data taken from NCES (1994) unless indicated above. Average Print Access Ranks were derived by taking the average of the ranks of Public Library Quality, School Library Quality, and Print at Home. An analysis using standardized scores to combine the three measures produced nearly identical results.

Table 7.7
Ranking of States on Print Access (by NAEP Score Rank)

STATE	NAEP READING RANK	AVERAGE PRINT ACCESS RANK	FREE READING RANK	NAEP SCORE (RAW)
New Hampshire	1	7	5	229
Maine	2	10	22	228
Iowa	4	4	1	227
Massachusetts	4	13	5	227
North Dakota	4	2	9	227
Wisconsin	6	4	5	225
New Jersey	8	9	35	224
Wyoming	8	5	20	224
Connecticut	9	6	20	223
Indiana	16	11	27	222
Minnesota	16	8	2	222
Nebraska	16	1	7	222
Pennsylvania	16	17	7	222
Utah	16	18	13	222
Virginia	16	15	13	222
Idaho	17	22	23	221
Missouri	17	14	13	221
Oklahoma	17	23	33	221
Ohio	19	20	22	219
Colorado	21	21	9	218
Rhode Island	21	25	13	218
Michigan	23	16	14	217
West Virginia	23	32	39	217
New York	24	12	20	216
Delaware	26	31	33	214
Kentucky	26	38	41	214
Texas	26	39	33	214
Georgia	29	36	20	213
North Carolina	29	26	25	213

Table 7.7 (con't)

STATE	NAEP READING RANK	AVERAGE PRINT ACCESS RANK	FREE READING RANK	NAEP SCORE (RAW)
Tennessee	29	37	28	213
Arkansas	32	29	37	212
Maryland	32	19	24	212
New Mexico	32	34	36	212
South Carolina	34	30	33	211
Arizona	35	27	33	210
Florida	36	33	35	209
Alabama	37	41	41	208
Louisiana	38	28	38	205
Hawaii	39	25	20	204
California	40	40	20	203
Mississippi	41	42	42	200
District of Columbia	42	36	27	189

Print access and free reading ranks are derived from the average of individual ranks computed as noted in Table 7.6. Standardized scores produced nearly identical results as those shown here. The averaged ranks were used in the correlational and multiple regression analyses. Again, the use of standardized scores produced virtually the same outcomes.

Table 7.8
Spearman Rank Order Correlations for Print Access, Free Reading, and NAEP Scores

	NAEP SCORE RANK	FREE READING RANK
Free Reading Rank	0.644	—
Average Print Access Rank	0.852	0.720

Table 7.9

Regression Analysis of Print Access and Poverty on NAEP Test Scores

VARIABLE	BETA	STANDARD ERROR	T	P VALUE
Constant	188.852	9.26	20.39	.000
Poverty	−.480	.094	−5.07	.000
Print Access	1.12	.260	4.30	.000

$R^2 = .72$, Adjusted $R^2 = .71$, F = 51.22

Table 7.10

Regression Analysis of Free Reading and Poverty on NAEP Test Scores

VARIABLE	BETA	STANDARD ERROR	T	P VALUE
Constant	167.16	40.55	4.12	.000
Poverty	−.615	.112	−5.48	.000
Free Reading	.68	.452	1.51	.140

$R^2 = .61$, Adjusted $R^2 = .59$, F = 31.23

strong and positive (r = .63), indicating that print access makes a powerful contribution to determining reading achievement in the states independent of socioeconomic factors.

Attempting to combine the effects of both print access and free reading statistically in a single analysis is more difficult with this particular set of data, since the variables are highly correlated, resulting in a fair degree of multicollinearity (Berry & Feldman, 1985; McQuillan, 1997a). This means that the variables are so interrelated that trying to tease out their specific, independent effects is problematic. A separate multiple regression analysis on the effects of poverty and print access on test scores was conducted, however. The regression analysis allows us to see if, taking into account both the effects of poverty and print access at the same time, each variable has a significant impact on test scores. As can be seen in Table 7.9, both variables do indeed make a distinct contribution to test scores (significant effects are indicated when the value of *P* is less than .05). Poverty is negatively related to reading scores, while print access has a significant positive influence on reading.

A similar analysis of poverty and free reading on reading scores (Table 7.10) shows, however, that free reading falls short of having a significant effect separate from poverty (p = .14). The free reading measure may fail to show an impact due to the restricted range in the measure itself: The mean score for free reading was 87.26 for the states (out of 100), with a standard deviation of only 2.27. There may not have been enough variation in the amount of free reading by state to produce an impact

Table 7.11
Intercorrelations among the Variables

	BOOKS	EXPENDITURES	SOFTWARE	PUBLIC LIBRARY	TEACHER-PUPIL
SAT-Verbal[a]	.29*	−.13	.01	.34*	−.11
Books		−.06	−.10	.10	−.37**
Expenditure			−.04	.17	−.20
Software				.09	.04
Public Library					.01

a = Partial correlations controlling for percent of students taking the SAT by state
* = p < .05, ** = p < .01

on test scores. Other state-level studies (Krashen, 1995) and analyses done with individual students (versus states, as in this case) have shown the effects of free reading separate from socioeconomic factors (Ortiz, 1986).

Print Access and Reading Achievement in High School: State SAT Verbal Scores

The powerful effects of print access extend beyond the elementary school level. A separate analysis (McQuillan, 1996a) of state SAT scores and library quality also shows the significant relationship between the availability of reading materials and reading comprehension. Using data from all fifty states and the District of Columbia (from Morgan, 1990; Podolsky, 1991; Snyder & Hoffman, 1990; and White, 1990), I calculated the correlation coefficients among the following variables: public library circulation per capita, school library holdings (books per pupil), teacher-pupil ratio, per pupil funding, computer software holdings, and an adjusted average score of the SAT Verbal scores for a state.[3]

Table 7.11 provides the intercorrelations for all the variables. Three relationships were significant: SAT scores were positively correlated with both the number of books per student in the school library and the per capita public library circulation, while the number of books per pupil was negatively correlated to the teacher-pupil ratio. It appears that states that have fewer library holdings also have more crowded classrooms. No other significant correlations were observed.

Table 7.12 shows the results of the multiple regression analysis, using the SAT Verbal scores (weighted for the percentage of students participating) as the dependent variable, with all predictor variables entered simultaneously. Not surprisingly, a measure of print access—public library circulation—was the only significant predictor of reading scores, with another—school library quality—falling just short of significance (p = .10). Once again, access shows itself to be an important predictor of reading achievement, even when controlling for such factors as per pupil spending, classroom size, and amount of computer software available.[4]

Table 7.12
Multiple Regression Analysis

PREDICTOR	B	BETA	STANDARD ERROR	T	P
Books	1.1500	.2339	.6946	1.65	.10
Expenditures	−.0032	−.1705	.0025	−1.23	.22
Software	.0338	.0732	.0622	.54	.58
Public Library	4.18	.3227	1.7664	2.36	.02
Teacher-Student	−1.0376	−.1070	1.3555	−.75	.45

$R^2 = .21$, adjusted $R^2 = .12$, $F = 2.44$, $p < .05$.

The Problem: Access Varies Enormously

Knowing the importance of print access on reading and reading achievement, it is only appropriate now to ask: How does access vary among students? The answer is that there are wide, sometimes dramatic disparities in print access among individual students, schools, and communities, and that these disparities result in large variations in achievement. Elley's (1994) study of reading achievement among more than 200,000 nine- and fourteen-year-old students in thirty-two countries discussed earlier found that the number of books available at home and in the school library varied significantly among students. Among the participating countries, the average number of books in the home varied from 25 to 174, and books per student in the school library from as few as 0.3 to as many as 28.9. In the United States, the mean number of books in the home was 137, but the standard deviation of 94 indicates considerable differences across the sample population. Similarly, the number of books per student in the school library in the United States was 19, but the standard deviation was 13.7, again indicative of huge disparities among schools. Data from large, nationally representative samples collected by the United States Department of Education corroborate these findings. The National Assessment of Educational Progress report (NCES, 1994), for example, found that the percentage of fourth graders reporting more than four types of reading materials in the home ranged from 25 percent to 46 percent among participating states.

Several smaller sample studies have found similar disparities in print access among children of varying ages at home, in school, and in the community. Halle and her colleagues (Halle et al., 1997) found considerable variability in the range of books present in the homes of African American children attending the inner-city school they studied, from a low of 4 to a high of 200 books per child, with the mean of 37.5 and a median of 29. Feitelson & Goldstein (1986) discovered large disparities between families (n = 102) from middle-class and lower-income backgrounds in schools where children were judged to be succeeding and doing poorly, respectively. The researchers visited each of the homes and counted the number of age-appropriate books in the homes. They discovered vast differences in the print access at home: a total of 2,774

Table 7.13

Book Access and Library Usage Among Lower- and Middle-Income Families

	LOW-INCOME	MIDDLE-INCOME
Number of Books Owned	13.75 (13.70)	35.40 (35.81)
Visits to Library/Month	3.72 (6.60)	9.30 (14.32)

(from Raz & Bryant, 1990, Table 5, p. 219.)

books for the 51 middle-class families (mean: 54.4) versus only 243 total for the poorly performing students (mean: 4.6)—ten times fewer books for the low-income families. The authors note that the differences are even greater than the mean and total figures indicate, as 61 percent of the low-income families had *no* books at all at home for their children. In addition, they observed that some of the books shown them and included in their count in the low-income families were not age appropriate—such as encyclopedia-type volumes kept in the family parlor—and were clearly not being used by even the older siblings in the household. In contrast, the middle-class homes, *with the economic resources to afford such items,* had books that showed considerable wear and tear and were easily accessible in the children's bedrooms.

Raz and Bryant (1990) also found definite differences in print access among middle-class and lower-income groups of children (n = 80) even before they began to read independently (ages four and five). Table 7.13 shows the differences they found. Note the large standard deviations indicated in the parentheses, showing that, although the two groups differed on average greatly (with three times as many books in the homes of middle- versus lower-income), considerable variation also was found within income groups. In another survey of preschool children's homes, Phillips and McNaughton (1990) found considerable variability in children's books in the homes of three- and four-year-olds among middle-class families in New Zealand. The average number of books found in the homes was 450, an astounding 300 of which were children's books, with a range of 50 to 500 per home.

One of the few studies to look systematically at home, school, and community print access for a single group of students was Smith, Constantino, and Krashen (1996). Smith et al. interviewed 40 students in low-income and high-income communities in the Los Angeles area. Children living in two economically depressed communities had respective averages of 0.4 and 2.67 age-appropriate books in the home; those living in the high-income district had *199.2.* The situation was similarly unequal at school and in the community: School libraries in the high-income community had around *three times* as many books per student, and public libraries had twice as many books per person.

LeMoine, O'Brian, Brandlin, and McQuillan (1997) found that disparities in access at home and in the community continue to exist within schools themselves. After surveying library access policies within and among school districts in southern California, the researchers found that students from high-achieving schools serving largely middle-class children allowed greater access to books, more time to read in

Table 7.14
Print Access in Urban and Suburban Schools

	SILENT READING TIME	1 VISIT PER WEEK TO LIBRARY	CAN TAKE BOOKS HOME	CAN MAKE INDEPENDENT VISITS TO LIBRARY
High-Achieving (Urban) n = 15	80% (12/15)	100% (15/15)	73% (11/15)	87% (13/15)
High-Achieving (Suburban) n = 8	100% (8/8)	100% (8/8)	100% (8/8)	86% (7/8)
Low-Achieving (Urban) n = 15	53% (8/15)	60% (9/15)	47% (7/15)	53% (8/15)

(from LeMoine et al., 1997, Table 1)

school, and more liberal check-out policies than those from lower-achieving schools in largely low-income neighborhoods. The results are summarized in Table 7.14.

Allington, Guice, Baker, Michaelson, and Li (1995) also surveyed school libraries in 12 high- and low-income neighborhoods in New York and found that high-income neighborhood schools had an average of 21.5 books per student, while low-income schools had only 15.4 volumes. Disparities among schools were also reported in magazine subscriptions, size of classroom libraries, and access policies. Similar inequalities in print access have also been documented in languages other than English at schools that serve a large number of language minority students (Pucci, 1994; Pucci & Ulanoff, 1996).[5]

A Print Wasteland: The Case of California

Ranking nearly last in the country in reading test scores, California provides a good case study of disparities in print access. While the state's policymakers have decided to focus their reform efforts on reading methodology (Stewart, 1996), there is good reason to believe that California's woes can be better traced to the abysmal state of its school and public libraries. California students now live in what can best be described as a print-barren desert and illustrate perfectly the situation John Holt alludes to in the quote at the beginning of this chapter: learning how to read but having nothing *to* read. The figures are sobering (McQuillan, in press: d):

> *California has some of the worst school libraries in the country.* Since children get anywhere from 30 to 90 percent of their free reading materials from the school and public library (Krashen, 1993), the health of a state's library system provides a good barometer of how well its students will do in literacy achievement. According to the most recent data available (White, 1990), California places last or nearly last in almost every category, including books per pupil, per pupil spending, and librarians per pupil. Table 7.15 shows just how far California is behind the na-

Table 7.15
School Library Quality in California and the United States

	ELEMENTARY	MIDDLE	HIGH SCHOOL
Books per Pupil			
U.S.	18:1	16:1	15:1
California	13:1	11:1	8:1
Per Pupil Spending			
U.S.	15.44	15.50	19.22
California	8.48	7.48	8.21
Librarians per Pupil	**Overall**		
U.S.	895:1		
California	5,496:1		

(from White, 1990; Snyder & Hoffman, 1995)

tional averages in library quality, and the state's rankings are telling: 45th in per-pupil expenditures, 49th in books per pupil, and 50th in librarians per pupil.

California has one of the worst public library systems in the United States. Similar to its poor standing in school libraries, California also ranks near the bottom on several measures of public library quality. In 1990–91, Chute (1992) reports that California ranked 39th in books and serials held per capita (1.95 versus 2.53 nationally), 43rd in capital outlay per 1,000 residents ($666.00 versus $1,912.00), and 50th in hours open to the public per 1,000 residents (72.09 hours/week). Not only does California rank relatively poorly now, but the situation has become far *worse* since the late 1980s. In 1993, Gibson noted that book budgets in the state had been cut 25 percent since 1989, the number of open hours had decreased 30 percent since 1987, and per capita spending had been reduced 36 percent from 1989. Children services had been the hardest hit, Gibson found, with 25% of public libraries reporting cutbacks in this area (Gibson, 1993).

California's children are poor and getting poorer. The only place children can find books outside of the school and public library is at home. But if you're poor, you're much less likely to be able to afford many books. California ranked 9th in the country in the number of children five- to seventeen-years old living in poverty (Bureau of the Census, 1995), with the poverty rate rising an incredible 25 percent in California between 1989 and 1993 (Schmittroth, 1994). According to the most recent figures, one out of every four California students is living in a family with income below the poverty line. Data gathered in the 1992 NAEP assessment confirm these figures: California ranked 10th highest among participating states in the number of children participating in free lunch and nutrition programs. Not surprisingly, the NAEP report also found that the state ranks near the bottom in the percentage of homes with more than 25 books in the home (NCES, 1994).

Education, Income, and the Problems of Measurement: What Access Isn't

As critical as understanding the influence of print access on reading frequency and achievement is, it is also important to understand what *doesn't* seem to influence access, at least directly, and discuss some issues related to how access is measured. A number of researchers, for example, have pointed out the influence of socioeconomic status (SES) (income, parental education) on academic achievement in general (White, 1983). Socioeconomic status and print access, while related, are not identical: There are children who live in middle-class families who have poor access to print, and those who live in low-income areas with a great deal of exposure to literacy. In addition, as Heath (1982) and Taylor and Dorsey-Gaines (1983) have pointed out, the literacy of families from diverse backgrounds is often different from that displayed in school, and many families in low socioeconomic areas have a great deal of reading and writing in their lives.

What seems instead to be the case is that children from low socioeconomic status homes often have less physical access *on average* to the kind of print materials related to the literacy most valued at school. As such, SES indicators serve as indirect but imperfect proxies for print access. But it is *not* low SES *per se* that is a barrier to literacy development, since those children who do have access to print and read frequently are successful in school. If this is indeed the case, then we should find that studies that provide both general measures of SES and specific measures of print access find that the two concepts are separate, and that print access has more predictive power in terms of reading proficiency.

Evidence from large-scale quantitative studies bears out this conclusion. Ortiz (1986), in an analysis of a large national data set on nearly 100,000 United States school children, found that students from low socioeconomic status families had fewer reading materials at home and were exposed to less reading in the home compared with students from more highly educated families, consistent with other research (Elley, 1996; Morrow, 1983; NCES, 1994). However, Ortiz also found that when controlled for level of SES, the impact of reading materials in the home and the extent of family reading was significant and substantial, suggesting that print in the environment was the critical variable affecting reading acquisition, not poverty or level of education.

White's (1983) metaanalysis of almost 200 studies on socioeconomic status and academic achievement provides evidence consistent with this hypothesized relationship. When studies examined SES and academic achievement with the individual student as the level of analysis, the strongest correlations with academic achievement were found with "home atmosphere" ($r = .58$), rather than income ($r = .31$) or education ($r = .19$). Studies which examined "home atmosphere" in White's analysis included in their definition a variety of variables, including reading materials in the home. Similarly, Okagaki, Frensch, and Gordon (1995) found that in a sample of low SES Latino youths, the high-achieving students came from significantly more literate environments than their less successful peers, again indicating that print access, not poverty itself, was one of the most critical determinants of academic achievement. As noted above, however, those in poverty are more likely to have more limited access to print than those who are not.

Rowe (1991, 1997) examined the effects of socioeconomic factors and reading behavior on the reading achievement of 5,000 students ages five to fourteen. He found that when home reading activities (reading alone, being read to, reading to others, and discussing reading), attitudes toward reading, and attentiveness at school were controlled for, socioeconomic status contributed very little to reading proficiency. This is again consistent with the notion that in and of itself, SES is not the crucial factor in reading achievement; rather, it is the actual amount of reading that counts. The most important implication of these findings is that we can improve the reading achievement of students in low SES schools by improving their access to print.

The "Try Harder" Solution: Mistaking Lack of Access for Lack of Effort

Some have argued that improving resources for students who currently lack them will not improve literacy, and that parental "values" or lack of effort are to blame for poor reading performance of students. Mayer (1997), for example, claims that the number of books a child has at home is only "weakly related" to parental income and that, because they cost so little, whether children have them depends largely "on parents' tastes and values" (p. 113). This conclusion must be interpreted with considerable caution.

Mayer's sample of children from National Longitudinal Study of Youth (NLSY) was restricted to four- and five-year-olds, most of whom were not likely to be independent readers (Durkin, 1966; McQuillan, in press: b). This alone might limit the generalizability of her findings for older students. More importantly, there were clear ceiling effects in her measure of the number of children's books in the home. Parents were asked to indicate the number of books their child possessed, from 1 to 10. Mayer's results are shown in Table 7.16.

The difference between poor and middle-income parents appears small, but this is most likely due to the ceiling effect for the middle 20 percent: the mean was 9.5 out of a maximum of 10. We know from the studies reviewed above on variability in access that 10 is probably well below the average number of books even in the homes of low-income families. Halle et al. (1997) found an average of more than 37 books per child in their study, and Phillips and McNaughton (1990) noted that their

Table 7.16
Number of Books Owned by Children Ages 4–5 by Income Percentile

POOREST 10%	MIDDLE 20%	ALL PARENTS
7.3	9.5	8.816

Standard Deviation = 2.557
(Mayer, 1997, pp. 108 and 187)

middle-class sample of parents had an *average* 300 children's books, or 30 times the maximum on the NLSY. In short, the scale used by Mayer is much too restricted to distinguish access differences among the sample population. The variability by income level is thus very likely to be underestimated by her analysis, as is its subsequent impact on tests of verbal ability and word recognition reported. (Although Mayer found that, even with this imperfect measure, the effect of print access as part of a larger index of "activities and possessions" in the home was still significant on the Peabody Picture Vocabulary Test (PPVT) even after controlling for mother's education, verbal ability, sex, and race [p. 111].) Mayer's additional claim that doubling the income of parents will not lead to a substantial increase in the number of books suffers from the same weakness of her percentile comparisons: A poor measure of books was used.

Sowell (1997) interprets Mayer's (1997) results to mean than, since "public libraries are free . . . [T]he big question is whether parents choose to take or send their children to such places" (p. C3), echoing Mayer's conclusions that parents could, if they wanted to, gain greater access to books for their children. But we have reviewed evidence that print access in poorer communities and schools is *substantially* worse than in middle-class communities, including public libraries (see also Di Loreto & Tse, in press). Access is thus *not* comparable or equally available for poor parents as it is to higher-income families. The presence or absence of certain "values" or effort is not sufficient for equaling the playing field among children, nor do they seem a very persuasive explanation for reading success and failure.[6]

Real Crises, Real Solutions

There is now considerable evidence that the amount and quality of students' access to reading materials is substantively related to the amount of reading they engage in, which in turn is the most important determinant of reading achievement. Many students attend schools where the level of print access is abysmal, creating a true crisis in reading performance. I do *not* wish to argue that simply providing books is all that is needed for schools to succeed, what some have referred to as the "garden of literacy" approach. Teaching is much more than physical resources, and no progress can be made without qualified and sensitive teachers. But just as we would not ask a doctor to heal without medicine, so we should not ask teachers and schools to teach without the materials to do so. Reading material is basic to all education, and providing a rich supply of reading matter to children of all ages, as well as a place and time to read, is the first step to bridging the gap between poor and good readers. This means that school libraries must be stocked with interesting and appealing materials and appropriately staffed; students need to be given time to read silently books of their own choosing (Krashen, 1993; Worthy, 1996); and states and communities need to fund public libraries with reading material for people of all backgrounds and interests. This seems to be a reasonable place to start in our efforts to provide all students with equal opportunities to reach high levels of literacy.

Endnotes

Endnotes for Chapter 1

1. Considerable debate has occurred over the levels of United States math and science performance, but even the sharpest critics of what Stedman (1997) calls the "new perspective" on school performance agree that no major declines in reading achievement in the United States have occurred over the past three decades (Stedman, 1996; Coulson, 1996). Critics have instead shifted their arguments to other grounds, to say in effect that "our top students aren't as good as they once were" (Coulson, 1996) or that our students have always performed at low levels (Stedman, 1996, 1997).

2. The NAEP report certainly encourages that interpretation. It proclaims that the cutoff scores "indicate if [students'] achievement meets expectations of what students *should know and should be able to do*" (Campbell, Donahue et al., 1996, p. 5).

3. This point was made to me by Gerald Coles (personal communication, 1997). See also Coles (1987).

4. Indeed, B. Shaywitz et al. (1992) found that the "dyslexic" children classified by the percentile method differed significantly from a comparison sample of "normal" readers in their mother's level of education (Table 3, p. 644). This suggests that environmental factors may be the cause of this supposed "dyslexia." Shaywitz et al. argued, however, that, after I.Q. is controlled for, mother's level of education had no impact on predicting reading scores. But mother's level of education, to the extent that it reflects the print environment at home, itself influences a child's I.Q., as Molfese, DiLalla, and Bunce (1997) demonstrate. Thus, I.Q. may act as a proxy for home environment, and controlling for it may attenuate the impact of the mother's level of education on reading scores. More careful measures of home environment are needed to rule out what appear from other research to be likely environmental influences on both I.Q. and reading.

5. Note that the whole problem of establishing "standards" and "minimal competencies" is not solved by, say, taking a "typical" fourth-grade curriculum and then asking if students can read the materials required. That only begs the question of how that "typical" curriculum was established in the first place (and by whom). And if you set your standard at the level that "most" fourth graders can handle, then we are back to square one, since we are no longer talking about what students *should* do, but what the average student can do, which is not a standard at all.

6. The specific relationship between age and reading proficiency is very strongly affected by how much one continues to read. Stanovich and his colleagues (Stanovich, West, & Harrison, 1995) found that their sample of older adults (average age = 79.9 years) did not have diminished vocabulary knowledge (a correlate of reading proficiency) when the amount of reading they did was taken into account. In other words, older adults who were active readers did no worse on reading measures than college students who had similar levels of reading experience. M. C. Smith's (1995) study of the NALS data showed that greater amounts of

reading is associated with higher reading proficiency at all age levels. Smith also found that level of educational attainment also predicts reading achievement, independent of current reading habits (pp. 214–215).

Comparisons across generations are, however, tricky at best, as Rothstein (1997) warns. Changes in tests, retention practices, the general education level of parents, and dropout rates all make direct comparisons very difficult. After an analysis of three large-scale testing programs over the past several decades, Rothstein concludes that "if there was a golden age of education from which we have fallen, we have no way of knowing about it because we have no way of making meaningful comparisons between achievement then and now" (p. 25).

7. Technically, the raw scores on commercial assessments such as the Iowa Test of Basic Skills are not directly comparable today to those of the 1950s, because the makers of the test "renorm" them every five to seven years. This means that the scale is readjusted so that half of the students score above the average and half below it. These average scores have generally been increasing each time the tests have been renormed over the last few decades, indicating a general rise in achievement for the student population on which they are calibrated.

8. Readers of the technical reports on the United States participation in the IEA study may come across one potentially fatal flaw in the composition of the United States nine-year-old sample, but it turns out there is little concern for alarm. Binkley, Williams, and Haynes (1994) report selected variables from the grade-four student questionnaire, including parental level of education. The results show that 48 percent of the nine-year-olds stated that their father had graduated from college, and 44 percent said their mother was a college graduate. These figures appear to be much too high, and, if true, would mean that the study vastly over-estimated United States reading proficiency by including a higher percentage of children from college-educated families than is found in the general student population or the United States population as a whole.

Fortunately, it is unlikely that these figures are correct. The IEA percentages represent the self-reports of nine-year-olds, who are likely to be inaccurate in their estimations of their parents' level of education. We know from a similar question asked on the NAEP reading survey that a large proportion (36 percent) of nine-year-olds state that they don't know their parent's level of education when given the option on a survey to say so. This is the problem with the IEA data: Students were not allowed to say they didn't know. They had to answer with something or leave the item blank. Binkley et al. (1994) report that only 9 percent of the nine-year-olds left the parental education items blank (p. 60), meaning that many of their responses were probably guesses.

One way of checking the accuracy of the nine-year-olds' answers are to compare them with the older students' responses, since they are more likely to know how much education their parents have had. The following table reports the responses of United States nine- and thirteen-year-olds on the IEA survey and the 1992 NAEP survey regarding parental level of education. (The IEA reports father's and mother's level of education separately; the NAEP survey has only one category: "parental" level. The "father" responses from the IEA results are used here, since they are consistently higher than those of the mother.)

It is clear from looking at the survey answers that failure to include a "don't know" option in the IEA survey of nine-year-olds probably resulted in an inaccurate estimation of parental education, but not necessarily a biased sample of students. The "true" number of students who are children of college graduates is around 41 percent, as indicated by the NAEP thirteen-year-old response. The results for the NAEP seventeen-year-olds are almost identical to the thirteen-year-olds, giving us more confidence that eighth-grade student responses are accurate.

Reported Level of Parents' Education in the 1991 IEA and 1992 NAEP Student Questionnaires

	9-YEAR-OLDS (GRADE 4)	13-YEAR-OLDS (GRADE 8)
IEA Study*:		
Less than H.S.	10%	(not
High School	24%	available)
Some College	18%	
College	48%	
I Don't Know	——	
NAEP Study:		
Less than H.S.	4%	8%
High School	12%	24%
Some College	9%	19%
College	39%	41%
I Don't Know	36%	8%

* = Father's level of education
Source: NCES (1994); Binkley et al. (1994).

Purves and Elley (1994) confirm that the parental education questions were found in an IEA pilot study to be inaccurate for the nine-year-olds in many countries (details of the study not given).

9. Murray and Herrnstein (1992) argue that the SAT declines of the 1960s and 1970s are, in fact, significant, since while not all college-bound seniors take the exam, all of those going to our "top" universities take them, and therefore declines are indicative of a serious drop in our academic "elite." This sounds persuasive until we consider just how many of the test takers are likely to go to the top colleges. There are more than 1 million college seniors who take the SAT. If we (rather generously) estimate that the top fifty colleges and universities each admit 2,000 freshmen, and all of these students only applied at one college each, that would still yield only 100,000 test takers, or about 10 percent of the entire pool. The average score, then, comes largely from those who do *not* attend the very best colleges and universities, and therefore we have no reason to suppose that top students are necessarily responsible for the small declines in SAT scores that have been noted. Unfortunately, information on self-reported class rank from test takers only became available in 1975, but the scores since that time indicate that students in the top fifth of their class experienced no declines (Carson, Huelskamp, & Woodall, 1993). Yet Murray and Herrnstein state that scores continued to "free-fall" from 1975 to 1980 among the country's best high school students.

Ironically, the critics who cite the SAT declines ignore the evidence of steady or rising graduate school admission scores that have taken place over the past two decades in the face of huge increases in the test pool (Berliner & Biddle, 1995). Presumably those who go on to graduate schools are the most able of those who attended college. The system that Murray and Herrnstein call the "mediocracy" which has resulted in "educational standards in the college track declin[ing] precipitously" (p. 51) has also produced students whose scores on the GRE have remained at record high levels. What is perhaps more unusual is that there is no mention in Murray and Herrnstein of the stable percentages of students at the highest levels of the one national test that actually is representative of all high school seniors, the NAEP.

10. A few nine-year-olds manage to score above 300 each year, but that figure, too, has held stable (1 percent in 1971, 1 percent in 1994). A few thirteen-year-olds have, for the first time in NAEP history, scored above the 350 level in 1992 and 1994 (1 percent each year), again indicating that, if anything, the number of students among the "best and the brightest" is higher now than ever before.

11. A creative analysis of some national test data collected by the United States Department of Education in 1972 and 1992 by a journalist with the *San Francisco Chronicle* (Marshall, 1997) reached essentially the same conclusions as my own review of the data in previous papers (McQuillan, 1996; in press: d), that test scores in California had not declined in recent years. Marshall used twelfth-grade reading scores from the National Longitudinal Survey (NLS) of 1972 and the National Educational Longitudinal Survey (NELS) of 1992. Although the state samples were not drawn randomly from the population, they were large enough (over 600 from 40 different California high schools in the NELS sample) to be, at the very least, suggestive of statewide trends. Using equated test scores from the two surveys, Marshall found that California's twelfth graders ranked about in the middle of states in 1992 when controlling for demographic variables such as parental level of education, income, and native language, and experienced no declines when compared to their counterparts in 1972.

12. Chall (1996) claims this interpretation of the NAEP scores is incorrect because "phonics is usually taught in grades 1 and 2, and possibly 3, [and] when it is taught in grade 4, it usually means that the students were already functioning below expectancy" (p. 305). In other words, low-scoring students in phonics classrooms are there because they are poor students to begin with. Chall argues that if we looked at the relationship between phonics and test scores in first and second grade, we would see higher scores for the phonics classrooms.

This interpretation is plausible if we looked only at the results nationally by individual classroom, as they are reported in NCES (1994). It is less persuasive, however, when we calculate the correlation between a state's NAEP score and a state's use of phonics in grade four, which turns out to also be very negative ($r = -.59$). If Chall (1996) were correct, it would mean that no meaningful correlation exists between what teachers of a given state do in reading instruction in fourth grade and what they do in the first three grades. In this case, it would mean that school districts with a strong emphasis on phonics in grade four don't necessarily use phonics in similar proportions in lower grades.

That is possible, of course, but not very likely. It seems much more probable that, on the whole, states, districts, and schools that use a lot of phonics in grade four also use a lot of phonics in grades one, two, and three. (Imagine if whole language backers used a similar argument in California—that the real problem was that the state's first, second, and third grade teachers were using phonics, and that the emphasis suddenly changed to whole language in grade four.) In any case, it may be that teaching methods have less to do with aggregate scores at the state level than other factors, such as access to reading materials (see Chapter 7).

There are other problems with the "blame whole language" argument based on the NAEP data. Very little reliable data exists on just how widely literature-based reading instruction was actually implemented in the state. The 1992 NAEP reading assessment reported that 69 percent of fourth-grade teachers in California said that they placed "heavy emphasis" on whole language practices in their classrooms, the highest percentage in the country. At the same time, 40 percent also said they gave "moderate emphasis" to phonics and 68 percent said they devoted at least some of their class time to decoding skills (NCES, 1994). Fisher and Hiebert (1990), in an analysis of teacher's self-reported labels concerning reading instruction and their observed reading practices, often found little correspondence between what teachers called themselves ("whole language," "phonics") and what went on in their classrooms. We should be cautious then, in making any strong claims about just how seriously whole language took root in California based on teacher self-reports.

Endnotes to Chapter 2

1. Despite various critiques of the details of Krashen's theory when first proposed to explain second-language acquisition (e.g., McLaughlin, 1978; Gregg, 1984), theorists generally agree that the reception of comprehensible input is critical in language acquisition, and that it accounts for a major portion of second-language competence (Larson-Freeman & Long, 1991; Van Patten, 1987).

2. I alone, of course, am responsible for the interpretation of Goodman's and Smith's ideas in this book.

3. Given a source of comprehensible input, the actual amount of listening or reading may be determined by other factors not represented in the model, such as affective variables. Krashen (1982) has also hypothesized that the reception of comprehensible input may not be sufficient for language acquisition to take place. There are also affective variables, such as self-esteem, motivation, and anxiety, that may affect the extent of acquisition (Dulay, Burt, & Krashen, 1982).

4. It is difficult to imagine, however, a case where at least some elaborative assistance would not be needed to help an acquirer understand oral or written messages.

Endnotes to Chapter 3

1. It is recognized, however, that children who can read independently can normally *also* recode, so that the ability to do the latter is at least related to the former, even if the relationship is not causal. Reading comprehension and recoding ability are clearly not identical, however. Children trained in phonemic awareness, for example, make large gains in tests of recoding but only small to moderate gains in reading comprehension (Krashen, 1996a; Bradley & Bryant, 1983), as we note in Chapter 5. Conversely, some adults classified as "dyslexic" show poor recoding ability and a slightly slower reading rate, but apparently normal passage comprehension (Elbro, Nielsen, & Petersen, 1994). Stothard and Hulme (1996) also provide evidence that some children who have difficulties in comprehension have normal recoding skills, and some poor decoders exhibit normal level of comprehension. Some second-language readers who have no problems in reading comprehension have low phonemic awareness (Holm & Dodd, 1997).

Differences exist in how phonological awareness is defined in the vast literature on the topic. Stanovich (1992), for example, proposes that we reject the term "awareness" completely and instead talk about a phonological continuum from "deep" to "shallow" types of "sensitivity" (see also Yopp, 1988). A task that required a child to match words based on rhyme (e.g., *talk* and *walk*) would tap a shallow level of sensitivity, whereas a test that required a child to delete or isolate a phoneme in a word (e.g., pronounce "cat" without the "cuh" sound) would indicate a deep level of sensitivity. Share (1995) appears to take the position that *phonemic* awareness of the "deep" kind is necessary for reading acquisition, and this is the definition I will use for this chapter.

2. Smith (1983) notes, however, the connection between sound and the meaning of words in oral vocabulary is no less arbitrary than between their written form and meaning, yet clearly we have sufficient memory for storing these associations for oral language.

3. It is interesting to note that many "beginning" children's books can only be understood by pre-readers if they are read to—that is, they are underspecified. The situation is much the same for beginning second-language readers, in that there is virtually nothing available commercially in print that would fall under our definition of "properly specified." To the extent that this is true for children's texts, the question of whether there is *independently* available comprehensible written language for early readers is still an open one.

4. McGee (1986) notes that Jones and Hendrickson (1970, cited in McGee) found that environmental print awareness developed before knowledge of print and book handling, indicating that it is one of the earliest encounters with text that children have. See also discussion of McGee et al. (1988) in text.

5. Note also that constantly pointing at the text while reading would very likely result in the children shifting their attention from meaning to form, and hence may be a quite "unnatural" type of exposure to print.

6. Other studies corroborate the findings of McGee et al. (1988) on the attention to graphic detail paid by very young children in identifying words in their environment. Hiebert (1978) found that preschool children had an awareness of print that extended to being able to distinguish where words began and ended in text, and Harste, Burke, and Woodward (1982) provide extensive evidence of pre-readers applying both "holistic" (use of extralinguistic cues) and "graphic" (use of letters) strategies in reading environmental print.

7. Heibert (1981) conducted longitudinal studies which she later reanalyzed (Heibert, Cioffi, & Antonak, 1984) in order to determine an order of reading concept acquisition. Her reanalysis found that the acquisition of letter name knowledge *preceded* knowledge of certain concepts of print. However, Lomax and McGee point out that the particular statistical procedure Heibert et al. used to arrive at that ranking involved rather stringent, "pass/fail" criteria for acquisition that might have missed more incremental changes (1987, p. 241).

Endnotes to Chapter 4

1. Cases are also known of children learning to read outside of school, often with little or no formal instruction, much *later* than their age peers. These "late readers" often make rapid progress once they begin reading, catching up to their peers within two years of learning how to read (Krashen & McQuillan, 1996; McQuillan, in press: b).

2. There are at least three other possible reasons for early reading intervention. First, it is argued that there exists a "Matthews Effect" for reading; that is, students who are behind in reading in first grade will fall further and further behind their age peers as they get older (Stanovich, 1986). Shaywitz and his colleagues (1995), however, have recently provided strong evidence that poor readers do *not* become worse relative to other readers as they progress through school, and in fact seem to make stronger gains as they get older, even when the data are adjusted for possible regression effects. Shaywitz et al. did find, though, that poor readers do not "catch up" to good readers, at least in the six years of data they analyzed (grades one to six), although they do begin to close the gap.

Second, early intervention supporters claim that bridging the gap between poor and good readers early will lead to eventual success in higher grades. It follows from this claim that it is important for children to be reading (or have related "reading skills") at grade level from the very beginning of their schooling. The evidence reviewed here on early reading does not support the assumption that early intervention is in fact sufficient for long-term reading success. Intensive "reading recovery" programs involving one-on-one tutoring in the early grades have had some success in affecting reading achievement in later grades, although the outcomes are rarely measured after more than a few grades (e.g., Pinnell, Lyons, Deford, Bryk, & Seltzer, 1994). It should also be noted that early intervention programs are very costly (Hiebert, 1994), so the efficiency of the program versus other, less expensive interventions must be considered.

Stanovich (1992) has stated that the initially small gains found in early intervention programs that emphasize phonemic awareness training (e.g., Bradley & Bryant, 1983) will have large, cumulative effects in the long run, countering claims by Yaden (1984; see also Krashen, 1996b) that such interventions may not warrant the effort expended on them. Unfortunately, the only experimental evidence Stanovich cites is an unpublished paper by Bryant in 1987, an apparent follow-up to his 1983 training study with Bradley.

Third, it is argued that the gap between poor and good readers cannot be bridged (or perhaps is more difficult to bridge) in the later grades. Some evidence exists, however, that just as early intervention is not sufficient, it may also not be necessary. M.C. Smith (1993) examined the reading performance of 87 adults twenty years after they graduated from high school. In a multiple regression analysis, he found that reading scores from grades nine and twelve accounted for a large portion (79 percent) of the variance in the subjects' current reading proficiency, but the addition of first-grade scores made no significant contribution to the variance explained. Smith's report does not specify whether first-grade reading scores were highly correlated with the scores from later grades, which, if true, would make his findings about the importance of the high school level reading scores somewhat less convincing. From Smith's presentation of the results, however, it appears as though a series of hierarchical regression analyses were conducted to compare the different amounts of variance accounted for by different grade levels, so that if the upper and lower grades were highly correlated, this effect would have shown up in his results. Smith's data suggest, then, that reading performance in the first grade is *not* critical for long-term success, and therefore that intervention made in later years may be more important than early-grade programs. It is also important to point out that the gap between "poor" and "good" readers in some of the longitudinal studies conducted is often not very large. In Juel (1988), for example, the poor readers were only slightly below grade level upon entry into middle school (3.5 at the end of fourth grade).

3. The results from a longitudinal study of an early intervention program reported in a recent paper (Leslie, Allen, & Calhoon, 1997) suggests this is indeed what happens. The researchers measured the fourth-grade reading achievement of a group of poor readers who received tutorial help in grades one through three. While all of the children were reading at grade level when they exited the early intervention program, almost half of them (47 percent) were below grade level again one to three years later. Early gains were not sustained. The results of this paper must be interpreted with caution, however, as a full report on the project has yet to be published. It is interesting to note that the intervention the children received in Leslie et al. (1997) consisted partly of asking the parents to read to their children, and sending home three to five books with the child after each tutoring session. A correlational analysis of third-grade reading scores and a variety of early literacy measures and intervention components found that these parental read-alouds were by far the strongest predictor of success ($r = .63$). This is consistent with the notion that elaborative assistance and book access are the most critical factors in reading achievement. A measure of phonological knowledge (rhyming ability), however, was not significantly correlated with later reading achievement ($r = .28$). It is not

known what sort of book access the children had once they exited the program and reached fourth grade, which may help explain their failure to remain at grade level in reading.

Endnotes for Chapter 5

1. Smith gives a good example of how reading is fundamentally "orthographic"—that is, a process of extracting meaning directly from the printed page without recourse to sound. Consider the following sentence:

> The none tolled hymn she had scene a pare of bear feat inn hour rheum.
>
> (Smith, 1973, p. 72)

You can very easily detect the misspelled words in this sentence, a good indication that we get meaning mostly from the visual properties of words, not their sound. If sound were the primary way of extracting meaning from text, there would be no reason to think anything was wrong with this sentence.

It has been said by some researchers (e.g., Horn & Manis, 1985; Stanovich, 1982) that good readers do not differ from poor readers in "orthographic processing," that is, the use of writing without making recourse to sound, or "phonological processing." However, Massaro and Sanocki (1993) point out that studies designed to measure orthographic information by breaking it down into smaller units, such as individual letters, as is typically done, do not give an accurate picture of the way orthographic knowledge is used in real reading, and hence will fail to detect potential differences. Barker et al. (1992) found that certain tasks tapping orthographic knowledge were much more strongly related to reading in elementary school children than the phonological tasks they used (phoneme deletion and pronouncing nonsense words).

2. See also Goodman (1996), Krashen (1998a), Moustafa (1997), Smith (1994), and Weaver (1994), for a discussion of many of these same issues.

3. It is also unclear just how well "concept of print" tests really measure print exposure. Morrow, O'Connor, and Smith (1990) found that kindergartners in traditional reading readiness and literature-based programs did not differ on the posttest results from one such test, Clay's Concepts about Print, but were significantly different on *other measures* of print exposure, including the amount of reading they did at home, the number of authors and book titles they could name, and the types of different reading material they could identify. These differences had an impact in literacy development: The literature-based classes did significantly better on two comprehension measures (story retelling and probed recall), as well as on their attempted readings of storybooks. The reading readiness groups did not, however, do significantly better on "skills" tests measuring auditory and visual discrimination and letter identification despite their additional training on these areas.

Endnotes to Chapter 6

1. It has been claimed by many researchers that Smith's position was that we actually "skipped" over letters and words, which I believe is not a correct interpretation of his position (see Smith, 1973, pp. 56–58). Smith noted that "words can be identified with only half the featural information that would be required if prior letter identification were necessary,

provided that features sampled are taken from different locations within the configuration" (p. 57); and "there will be many alternative 'critical sets' of about 15 features per word, provided the features are a sampling from all the locations [in the word]" (p. 57). There is no implication that letters will necessarily be skipped over, as subletter features may be sampled from the entire array of the visual stimulus—that is, possibly from all the letters of the word.

2. Identification of individual words may take place after the eye has scanned across them and after we identify meaning, as is the case with individual letters in a word. See Smith (1994) for a more thorough treatment of this topic.

3. Of course, as reading proficiency increases, both decoding ability and context facilitation may lead to fewer errors of all types for both good and poor readers on a relatively easy passage. The skilled readers in Stanovich et al. (1984) scored at a grade equivalent of 2.9 in the spring, while the text had a readability level of grade one. As expected, skilled readers made virtually no errors on the passage when tested in the spring (0.8 errors on the coherent paragraph). Good readers will be both more accurate *and* better users of context than poor readers when the situation warrants.

4. Smith (1994), commenting on the context studies by Stanovich and others, notes that the entire argument may be misplaced: His own conception of "context" extends far beyond the words on the page and is mostly that which is in the reader's mind, the "nonvisual" information we possess.

5. One vote given for each measure included on Chall's Table 4-1A and 4-1B (combining first and second grades). I have adjusted the count to reflect the errors Carbo (1988) pointed out in Chall's analysis. Chall (1989), in responding to Carbo, did not contest the errors in her analysis of these particular cases.

6. Morrow conducted another literature-based study at the kindergarten level that is not included here, since the children had not yet begun to read independently (Morrow, O'Connor, & Smith, 1990). It is interesting to note, however, that those exposed to more print did much better in story comprehension as well as the amount and types of reading they did at home, demonstrating the effects of print exposure even before independent reading. Morrow et al. compared the effects of extensive print exposure through a storybook reading in eight "at-risk" kindergarten classrooms. Four of the classes engaged in traditional reading readiness activities, quiet book reading, read-alouds, retellings and repeated readings of stories, and other literature-related activities. The four control classes had significantly less exposure to print, and instead used a "reading readiness" program that focussed on letters of the alphabet as well as some storybook reading. The researchers made weekly observations of the classrooms to ensure treatment fidelity of the literature-based component, which lasted about 60 minutes per day. Two tests of comprehension were administered (story retelling and probed recall), on which the experimental groups did significantly better. The children in the literature-based classes were also able to name more book titles and authors, and reported a greater amount of reading at home (pp. 266–267).

7. In addition to increasing student access to books, the programs that Gambrell (1996) evaluated also used some incentives (bookmarks and books) to motivate the children to read more. It is not clear that these incentives were critical to the programs' success, however, since there was no control group that received increased access to books but no rewards. In previous studies, access to books alone has been found effective in increasing reading frequency (Krashen, 1993); incentives alone have not (McQuillan, 1997b). Incentives have not been found to increase motivation in other academic areas (Kohn, 1993), and in fact can have a negative impact on both motivation and achievement (Deci & Ryan, 1992).

Endnotes for Chapter 7

1. One apparent counterexample to the experimental evidence on the positive effects of more reading and book access is Carver and Leibert (1995), whose subjects did not seem to improve in reading after an seven-week summer "free reading" session. The study had numerous flaws, however, that make the results completely understandable, even predictable. The most serious error was that students were not allowed to read any books even slightly above their predetermined grade level! This restriction itself almost guaranteed that no progress in reading comprehension or vocabulary would be made. In addition, the students had a very small number of books to choose from, again limiting their ability to read voluminously enough to benefit from the time spent in the program.

2. This approach was recommended to me by Stephen Krashen.

3. Since a state's mean SAT score is very strongly and negatively related to the percentage of total high school students taking the exam ($r = -.86$), this percentage was used as a weighting variable in the analysis to control for this source of bias in the scores.

4. It may be somewhat surprising to some that school expenditures did not directly predict reading scores among high school students. The situation is more complicated than what is represented in this analysis. Lance et al. (1993), in a more sophisticated path analysis of access and reading at the district level in Colorado, found that spending did affect reading achievement in so far as it has an impact on the collections of the school library. A more detailed examination of the relationship between total spending and library expenditures is needed to confirm this finding at the national level. Similarly, class size as determined by teacher-student ratio did not by itself predict high school reading achievement. Again, Lance et al. found that such a relationship was mediated by the school library: Teacher-student ratio was related to school library-media center size, which in turn predicted academic achievement. The significant correlation in the current study between teacher-student ratio and books per pupil supports Lance et al.'s finding, in that the larger the average classroom, the fewer the number of books per student in the school library.

5. Martinez and her colleagues (Martinez, Roser, Worthy, Strecker, & Gough, 1997) point out that the notion of "access" should include not merely the number of books physically present in a given location, but the readability and interest of the texts themselves. In their study of three low-socioeconomic-status classroom libraries, they found that many of the books in the classroom were not read (or likely to be read) by the children precisely because they were too difficult for them. They also noted that many others were "dated, worn . . . and inappropriate in other ways" (p. 271).

6. I will speculate that there is one sense in which the "try harder" solution is correct and can even be demonstrated by cases of those who have "pulled themselves up by their own bootstraps." This is because if you lack the proper resources, extraordinary measures are the *only* way to succeed (although they still may be insufficient). It is thus not surprising to find media stories about the occasional student who "makes it" attending a poorly funded school, and (rightly) points to his or her own heroic efforts and determination. How *else* could he or she have succeeded? Rather than make the case that effort is the essential ingredient, these cases demonstrate how difficult such a feat really is compared to that routinely performed by those who come from more advantaged backgrounds. Applying such Herculean efforts, then, is not the path taken by the typical child of most middle- and upper-income families. As the old joke goes, we shouldn't confuse being born on third base with hitting a triple (thanks to Stephen Krashen for this last observation).

References

Adams, M. (1990). *Beginning to read: Thinking and learning about print.* Cambridge, MA: The MIT Press.

Allington, R. (1983). The reading instruction provided readers of differing abilities. *Elementary School Journal, 83,* 548–559.

Allington, R., Guice, S., Baker, K., Michaelson, N., & Li, S. (1995). Access to books: Variations in schools and classrooms. *The Language and Literacy Spectrum, 5,* 23–25.

Anderson, R., Wilson, P., & Fielding, L. (1988). Growth in reading and how children spend their time outside of school. *Reading Research Quarterly, 23,* 285–303.

Asher, J. (1994). *Learning another language through actions,* 4th edition. Los Gatos, CA: Sky Oaks Productions.

Ball, E., & Blachman, B. (1991). Does phonemic awareness training in kindergarten make a difference in early word recognition and developmental spelling? *Reading Research Quarterly, 26,* 49–66.

Banks, S., Guyer, B., & Guyer, K. (1995). A study of medical students and physicians referred for learning disabilities. *Annals of Dyslexia, 45,* 233–245.

Barker, T., Torgesen, J., & Wagner, R. (1992). The role of phonological processing skills on five different reading tasks. *Reading Research Quarterly, 27,* 334–345.

Bentin, S., Hammer, R., & Cahan, S. (1991). The effects of aging and first grade schooling on the development of phonological awareness. *Psychological Science, 2*(4), 271–274.

Berliner, D., & Biddle, B. (1995). *The manufactured crisis: Myths, fraud, and the attack on America's public schools.* Reading, MA: Addison-Wesley Publishing.

Berry, W., & Feldman, S. (1985). *Multiple regression in practice.* Newbury Park, CA: Sage Publications.

Binkley, M., & Williams, T. (1996). *Reading literacy in the United States: Findings from the IEA reading literacy study.* Washington, D.C.: National Center for Educational Statistics.

Binkley, M., Williams, T., & Haynes, J. (1994). Constructs and data. In M. Binkley & K. Rust (Eds.), *Reading literacy in the United States: Technical report of the U.S. component of the IEA reading literacy study* (pp. 243–348). Washington, D.C.: National Center for Educational Statistics.

Blumenfeld, S. (1995). *The whole language/OBE fraud: The shocking story of how America is being dumbed-down by its own education system.* Boise, ID: Paradigm Company.

Bracey, G. (1997a). *Setting the record straight: Responses to misconceptions about public education in the United States.* Alexandria, VA: Association for Supervision and Curriculum Development.

Bracey, G. (1997b). The seventh Bracey report on the condition of public education. *Phi Delta Kappan, 79,* 120–137.

Bradley, B. (1956). An experimental study of the readiness approach to reading. *The Elementary School Journal, 56,* 262–267.

Bradley, L., & Bryant, P. (1983). Categorizing sounds and learning to read—a causal connection. *Nature (London), 301,* 419–421.

Brenna, B. (1995). The metacognitive reading strategies of five early readers. *Journal of Research in Reading, 18,* 53–62.

Briggs, C., & Elkind, D. (1977). Characteristics of early readers. *Perceptual and Motor Skills, 44,* 1231–1237.

Brown, R. (1973). *A first language: The early stages.* Cambridge, MA: Harvard University Press.

Bruck, M. (1990). Word recognition skills of adults with childhood diagnoses of dyslexia. *Developmental Psychology, 26,* 439–454.

Bureau of the Census. (1995). *Statistical abstract of the United States.* Washington, D.C.: U.S. Department of Commerce.

Byrne, B. (1992). Studies in the acquisition procedure for reading: Rationale, hypotheses, and data. In P. Gough, L. Ehri, & R. Treiman (Eds.), *Reading acquisition* (pp. 1–34). Hillsdale, NJ: Lawrence Erlbaum Associates.

Byrne, B., & Fielding-Barnsley, R. (1989). Phonemic awareness and letter knowledge in the child's acquisition of the alphabetic principle. *Journal of Educational Psychology, 81,* 313–321.

Byrne, B., & Fielding-Barnsley, R. (1993). Evaluation of a program to teach phonemic awareness to young children: A 1-year follow-up. *Journal of Educational Psychology, 85,* 104–111.

California Reading Task Force Report (CRTFR). (1995). *Every child a reader.* Sacramento, CA: California Department of Education.

Campbell, D., & Stanley, J. (1966). *Experimental and quasi-experimental designs for research.* Chicago: Rand McNally.

Campbell, J., Donahue, P., Reese, C., & Phillips, G. (1996). *NAEP 1994 reading report card for the nation and the states.* Washington, D.C.: U.S. Department of Education.

Campbell, J., Reese, C., O'Sullivan, C., & Dossey, J. (1996). *NAEP 1994 trends in academic progress.* Washington, D.C.: National Center for Educational Statistics.

Campbell, J., Voelkl, K., & Donahue, P. (1997). *NAEP 1996 trends in academic progress.* Washington, D.C.: National Center for Education Statistics.

Campbell, R. (1991). The importance of special cases: Or how the deaf might be, but are not, phonological dyslexics. *Mind and Language, 6,* 107–112.

Carbo, M. (1988). Debunking the great phonics myth. *Phi Delta Kappan, 70*(3), 226–240.

Carnine, D. (1977). Phonics versus look-say: Transfer to new words. *Reading Teacher, 30,* 636–640.

Carson, C., Huelskamp, R., & Woodall, T. (1993). Perspectives on education in America: An annotated briefing, April, 1992. *Journal of Educational Research, 86,* 261–310.

Carver, R., & Leibert, R. (1995). The effect of reading library books at different levels of difficulty upon gains in reading ability. *Reading Research Quarterly, 30,* 26–48.

Chall, J. (1967/1983). *Learning to read: The great debate.* New York: McGraw-Hill.

Chall, J. (1989). Learning to read: The great debate 20 years later: A response to "Debunking the great phonics myth." *Phi Delta Kappan, 70*(7), 521–538.

Chall, J. (1996). American reading achievement: Should we worry? *Research in the Teaching of English, 30,* 303–310.

Chute, A. (1992). *Public libraries in the United States, 1990.* Washington, D.C.: U.S. Department of Education.

Cipielewski, J., & Stanovich, K. (1992). Predicting growth in reading ability from children's exposure to print. *Journal of Experimental Child Psychology, 54,* 74–89.

Coles, G. (1987). *The learning mystique: A critical look at "learning disabilities."* New York: Pantheon Books.

Coltheart, M. (1979). When can children learn to read and when should they be taught? In G. Waller & G. Mackinnon (Eds.), *Reading research: Advances in theory and practice,* Vol. 1 (pp. 1–30). New York: Academic Press.

Cossu, G., Rossini, F., & Marshall, J. (1993). When reading is acquired but phonemic awareness is not: A study of literacy in Down's syndrome. *Cognition, 46,* 129–138.

Coulson, A. (1996). Schooling and literacy over time: The rising cost of stagnation and decline. *Research in the Teaching of English, 30,* 311–327.

Cross, T. (1977). Mothers' speech adjustments: The contributions of selected child listener variables. In C. Snow & C. Ferguson (Eds.), *Talking to children: Language input and acquisition* (pp. 151–188). London: Longman.

Cunningham, A. (1990). Explicit versus implicit instruction in phonemic awareness. *Journal of Experimental Child Psychology, 50,* 429–444.

Cunninghan, A., & Stanovich, K. (1990). Assessing print exposure and orthographic processing skill in children: A quick measure of reading experience. *Journal of Educational Psychology, 82,* 733–740.

Cunningham, A., & Stanovich, K. (1993). Children's literacy environments and early word recognition skills. *Reading and Writing: An Interdisciplinary Journal, 5,* 193–204.

Deci, E., & Ryan, R. (1992). The initiation and regulation of intrinsically motivated learning and achievement. In A. Boggiano & T. Pittman, (Eds.), *Achievement and motivation: A social-developmental perspective* (pp. 9–36). Cambridge: Cambridge University Press.

Di Loreto, C., & Tse, L. (in press). Seeing is believing: Disparity of books in two Los Angeles area public libraries. *Public Library Quarterly.*

Dorrell, L., & Carroll, E. (1981). Spider-Man in the library. *School Library Journal, 27,* 17–19.

Dulay, H., Burt, M., & Krashen, S. (1982). *Language two.* New York: Oxford.

Durkin, D. (1966). *Children who read early.* New York: Teachers College Press.

Durkin, D. (1974–1975). A six year study of children who learned to read in school at the age of four. *Reading Research Quarterly, 10,* 9–61.

Education Week. (1997, January 15). Comparing test results. Online: http://www.edweek.org.

Ehri, L. (1992). Reconceptualizing the development of sight word reading and its relationship to recoding. In P. Gough, L. Ehri, & R. Treiman (Eds.), *Reading acquisition* (pp. 107–144). Hillsdale, NJ: Lawrence Erlbaum Associates.

Ehri, L., & Sweet, J. (1991). Fingerpoint-reading of memorized text: What enables beginners to process the print? *Reading Research Quarterly, 26,* 442–462.

Ehri, L., & Wilce, L. (1985). Movement into reading: Is the first stage of printed word learning visual or phonetic? *Reading Research Quarterly, 20,* 163–179.

Ehri, L., & Wilce, L. (1987a). Does learning to spell help beginners learn to read words? *Reading Research Quarterly, 22,* 47–65.

Ehri, L., & Wilce, L. (1987b). Cipher and cue reading: An experiment in decoding acquisition. *Journal of Educational Psychology, 79,* 3–13.

Elbro, C., Nielsen, I., & Petersen, D. (1994). Dyslexia in adults: Evidence for deficits in nonword reading and in the phonological representations of lexical items. *Annals of Dyslexia, 44,* 205–226.

Eldredge, L. (1991). An experiment with a modified whole language approach in first-grade classrooms. *Reading Research and Instruction, 30,* 21–38.

Elley, W. (1991). Acquiring literacy in a second language: The effect of book-based programs. *Language Learning, 41,* 375–411.

Elley, W. (1992). *How in the world do students read? The IEA study of reading literacy.* The Hague, Netherlands: International Associations for the Evaluation of Educational Achievement.

Elley, W. (1994). Preface. In W. Elley (Ed.), *The IEA study of reading literacy: Achievement and instruction in thirty-two school systems* (pp. xxi–xxii). Oxford, England: Pergamon.

Elley, W. (1996). Lifting literacy levels in developing countries: Some implications from an IEA study. In V. Greaney (Ed.), *Promoting reading in developing countries: Views on making read-*

ing materials accessible to increase literacy levels (pp. 39–54). Newark, DE: International Reading Association.

Elley, W. (1997, June). *Reading in the present world: Realities and possibilities.* Paper presented at the 2nd Conference on Functional Literacy, Amsterdam.

Elley, W., & Mangubhai, F. (1983). The impact of reading on second language learning. *Reading Research Quarterly, 19,* 53–67.

Elley, W., Schleicher, A., & Wagemaker, H. (1994). Introduction. In W. Elley (Ed.), *The IEA study of reading literacy: Achievement and instruction in thirty-two school systems,* (pp. 1–34). Oxford, England: Pergamon.

Evans, M., & Carr, T. (1985). Cognitive abilities, conditions of learning, and the early development of reading skill. *Reading Research Quarterly, 20,* 327–350.

Feitelson, D., & Goldstein, Z. (1986). Patterns of book ownership and reading to young children in Israeli school-oriented and nonschool-oriented families. *Reading Teacher, 39,* 924–930.

Finn, P. (1977–1978). Word frequency, information theory, and cloze performance: A transfer feature theory of processing reading. *Reading Research Quarterly, 13,* 508–537.

Fisher, C., & Hiebert, E. (1990). Characteristics of tasks in two approaches to literacy instruction. *Elementary School Journal, 91,* 3–18.

Foorman, B., Francis, D., Beeler, T., Winikates, D., and Fletcher, J. (in press). Early interventions for children with reading problems: Study designs and preliminary findings. *Learning Disabilities: A Multi-Disciplinary Journal.*

Forester, A. (1977). What teachers can learn from "natural readers." *Reading Teacher, 31,* 160–166.

Freed, B. (1980). Talking to foreigners versus talking to children: Similarities and differences. In R. Scarcella & S. Krashen (Eds.), *Research in second language acquisition* (pp. 19–27). Rowley, MA: Newbury House.

Freppon, P. (1991). Children's concepts of the nature and purpose of reading in different instructional settings. *Journal of Reading Behavior, 23,* 139–163.

Freppon, P. (1995). Low-income children's literacy interpretations in a skills-based and a whole-language classroom. *Journal of Reading Behavior, 27,* 505–533.

Gambrell, L. (1996). Creating classroom cultures that foster reading motivation. *Reading Teacher, 50,* 14–25.

Gaskins, I., Ehri, L., Cress, C., O'Hara, C., & Donnelly, K. (1996). Procedures for word learning: Making discoveries about words. *Reading Teacher, 50,* 312–327.

Gibson, L. (1993). *Status of California public libraries: Final report, abbreviated version.* Sacramento, CA: California State Library.

Glass, G. (1978). Standards and criteria. *Journal of Educational Measurement, 15,* 237–261.

Gollash, F. (Ed.) (1982). *Language and literacy: The selected works of Kenneth S. Goodman.* London: Routledge & Kegan Paul.

Goodman, K. (1965). A linguistic study of cues and miscues in reading. *Elementary English, 42,* 639–643.

Goodman, K. (1967). Reading: A psycholinguistic guessing game. *Journal of the Reading Specialist, 6,* 126–135.

Goodman, K. (1971). Decoding, from code to what? *Journal of Reading, 14,* 445–462.

Goodman, K. (1996). *On reading.* Portsmouth, NH: Heinemann.

Goodman, K., & Goodman, Y. (1979). Learning to read is natural. In L. Resnick & P. Weaver (Eds.), *Theory and practice in early reading,* Vol. 1 (pp. 137–154). Hillsdale, NJ: Lawrence Erlbaum Associates.

Goodman, K., & Goodman, Y. (1982). Spelling ability of a self-taught reader. In F. Gollasch (Ed.), *Language and literacy: The selected works of Kenneth S. Goodman,* Vol. 2 (pp. 221–226). London: Routledge & Kegan Paul.

Goodman, Y. (1986). Children coming to know literacy. In W. Teale & E. Sulzby (Eds.), *Emergent literacy: Writing and reading* (pp. 1–14). Norwood, NJ: Ablex Publishing.

Goswami, U., & Bryant, P. (1990). *Phonological skills and learning to read.* East Sussex, England: Lawrence Erlbaum Associates.

Gough, P., & Hillinger, M. (1980). Learning to read: An unnatural act. *Bulletin of the Orton Society, 30,* 179–196.

Gray, S. & Klaus, R. (1970). The early training project: A seventh-year report. *Child Development, 41,* 909–924.

Gregg, K. (1984). Krashen's monitor and Occam's razor. *Applied Linguistics, 5,* 79–100.

Guthrie, J., Kirst, M., Hayward, G., Odden, A., Adams, J., Cagampang, H., Emmett, T., Evans, J., Geranios, J., Koppich, J., & Merchant, B. (1988). *Conditions of education in California, 1987–88.* Berkeley, CA: Policy Analysis for California Education.

Guthrie, J., Kirst, M., Koppich, J., Hayward, G., Odden, A., Rahn, M., & Wiley, L. (1993). *Conditions of education in California, 1992–93.* Berkeley, CA: Policy Analysis for California Education.

Hagerty, P., Hiebert, E., & Owens, M. (1989). Students' comprehension, writing, and perceptions in two approaches to literacy instruction. In S. McCormick & J. Zutell, *Cognitive and social perspectives in literacy research and instruction: Thirty-eighth yearbook of the National Reading Conference* (pp. 453–459). Chicago: National Reading Conference.

Halle, T., Kurtz-Costes, B., & Mahoney, J. (1997). Family influences on school achievement in low-income, African American children. *Journal of Educational Psychology, 89,* 527–537.

Halliday, M. (1969). Relevant models of language. *Educational Review, 22,* 1–128.

Hanson, R., & Farrell, D. (1995). The long-term effects on high school seniors of learning to read in kindergarten. *Reading Research Quarterly, 30,* 908–933.

Harris, A., & Serwer, B. (1966). The CRAFT Project: Instructional time in reading research. *Reading Research Quarterly, 2,* 1–56.

Harste, J., Burke, C., & Woodward, V. (1982). Children's language and the world: Initial encounters with print. In J. Langer & M.T. Smith-Burke (Eds.), *Reader meets author/bridging the gap* (pp. 105-131). Newark, DE: International Reading Association.

Hart, B., & Risley, T. (1995). *Meaningful differences in the early experiences of young American children.* Baltimore: Paul H. Brookes Publishing.

Hatcher, P., Hulme, C., & Ellis, A. (1994). Ameliorating early reading failure by integrating the teaching of reading and phonological skills: The phonological linkage hypothesis. *Child Development, 65,* 41-57.

Heath, S. (1982). *Ways with words.* Cambridge: Cambridge University Press.

Henderson, S., Jackson, N., & Mukamal, R. (1993). Early development of language and literacy skills of an extremely precocious reader. *Gifted Child Quarterly, 37,* 78–84.

Hiebert, E. (1978). Preschool children's understanding of written language. *Child Development, 49,* 1231–1234.

Hiebert, E. (1981). Developmental patterns and interrelationships of preschool children's print awareness. *Reading Research Quarterly, 16,* 236–259.

Hiebert, E. (1994). Reading recovery in the United States: What difference does in make to an age cohort? *Educational Researcher, 23,* 15–25.

Hiebert, E., Cioffi, G., & Antonak, R. (1984). A developmental sequence in preschool children's acquisition of reading readiness skills and print awareness concepts. *Journal of Applied Developmental Psychology, 5,* 115–126.

Hirsch, E. D. (1996). *The schools we need and why we don't have them.* New York: Doubleday.

Holm, A., & Dodd, B. (1997). The effect of first written language on the acquisition of English literacy. *Cognition, 59,* 119–147.

Holt, J. (1972/1993). *Freedom and beyond.* Portsmouth, NH: Heinemann.

Horn, C., & Manis, F. (1985). Normal and disabled readers' use of orthographic structure in processing print. *Journal of Reading Behavior, 17,* 143–161.

Jackson, N. (1988). Precious reading ability: What does it mean? *Gifted Child Quarterly 32,* 200–204.

Jackson, N. & Lu, W. (1992). Bilingual precocious readers of English. *Roeper Review, 14,* 115–119.

Juel, C. (1988). Learning to read and write: A longitudinal study of 54 children from first through fourth grades. *Journal of Educational Psychology, 80,* 437–447.

Juel, C., Griffith, P., & Gough, P. (1986). Acquisition of literacy: A longitudinal study of children in first and second grade. *Journal of Educational Psychology, 78,* 243–255.

King, E., & Friesen, D. (1972). Children who read in kindergarten. *Alberta Journal of Educational Research, 18,* 147–161.

Kirsch, I., Jungblut, A., Jenkins, L., & Kolstad, A. (1993). *Adult literacy in America: A first look at the results of the National Adult Literacy Survey.* Washington, D.C.: National Center of Educational Statistics.

Klesius, J., Griffith, P., & Zielonka, P. (1991). A whole language and traditional instruction comparison: Overall effectiveness and development of the alphabetic principle. *Reading Research and Instruction, 30,* 47–61.

Knapp, M., Adelman, N., Marder, C., McCollum, H., Needels, M., Padilla, C., Shields, P., Turnbull, B., & Zucker, A. (1995). *Teaching for meaning in high-poverty classrooms.* New York: Teachers College Press.

Kohn, A. (1993). *Punished by rewards.* Boston: Houghton Mifflin Company.

Krashen, S. (1976). Formal and informal linguistic environments in language learning and language acquisition. *TESOL Quarterly, 10,* 157–168.

Krashen, S. (1981). *Second language acquisition and second language learning.* New York: Prentice Hall.

Krashen, S. (1982). *Principles and practice in second language acquisition.* New York: Prentice Hall.

Krashen, S. (1985). *The input hypothesis: Issues and implications.* London: Longman.

Krashen, S. (1989). We acquire vocabulary and spelling by reading: Additional evidence for the Input Hypothesis. *Modern Language Journal, 73,* 440–464.

Krashen, S. (1993). *The power of reading.* Englewood, CO: Libraries Unlimited.

Krashen, S. (1995). School libraries, public libraries, and the NAEP reading scores. *School Library Media Quarterly, 23,* 235–236.

Krashen, S. (1996a). *Every person a reader: An alternative to the California's Reading Task Force Report.* Culver City, CA: Language Education Associates.

Krashen, S. (1996b). *Issues in literacy development.* Testimony presented to the California Framework on Language Arts Committee, October 25, 1996, Sacramento, CA.

Krashen, S. (1997a). *The secrets of phonemic awareness.* Unpublished manuscript, University of Southern California. Los Angeles, CA.

Krashen, S. (1998a). Some problems with "Informed instruction for reading success: Foundations for teacher preparation." *California English, 31*(2), 6–12.

Krashen, S. (1998b). Eye fixation studies do not disprove the Goodman-Smith hypothesis. In P. Dreyer (Ed.), *Sixty-first yearbook of the Claremont Reading Conference.* Claremont, CA: Claremont Reading Conference.

Krashen, S., & McQuillan, J. (1996). *The case for late intervention: Once a good reader, always a good reader.* Culver City, CA: Language Education Associates.

Lance, K., Wellborn, L., & Hamilton-Pennell, C. (1993). *The impact of school library media centers on academic achievement.* Castle Rock, CO: Hi Willow Research and Publishing.

Larsen-Freeman, D., & Long, M. (1991). *Introduction to second language acquisition research.* London: Longman.

Lee, S., & Krashen, S. (1996). Free voluntary reading and writing competence in Taiwanese high school students. *Perceptual and Motor Skills, 83,* 687–690.

Lee, S., Krashen, S., & Tse, L. (1997). The author recognition test and vocabulary knowledge: A replication study. *Perceptual and Motor Skills, 85,* 1428–1430.

LeMoine, N., O'Brian, B., Brandlin, E., & McQuillan, J. (1997). The (print-) rich get richer: Library access in low- and high-achieving elementary schools. *California Reader, 30,* 23–25.

Leslie, L., Allen, L., & Calhoon, A. (1997, November). *How are they doing? A follow-up study of at-risk children who participated in an early intervention project.* Paper presented at the National Reading Conference, Scottsdale, Arizona.

Levine, A. (1996, October). America's reading crisis: Why the whole-language approach to teaching has failed millions of children. *Parents, 16,* 63–65 and 68.

Lie, A. (1991). Effects of a training program for stimulating skills in word analysis in first-grade children. *Reading Research Quarterly, 26,* 234–250.

Light, R., & Pillemer, D. (1984). *Summing it up: The science of reviewing research.* Cambridge, MA: Harvard University Press.

Lomax, R., & McGee, L. (1987). Young children's concepts about print and reading: Toward a model of word reading acquisition. *Reading Research Quarterly, 22,* 237–256.

Lundberg, I., Frost, J., & Petersen, O. (1988). Effects of an extensive program for stimulating phonological awareness in preschool children. *Reading Research Quarterly, 23,* 263–284.

Marshall, J. (1997, September 9). California student achievement, 1972 to 1992: Technical notes. *San Francisco Chronicle,* p. A1 [on-line edition].

Marshall, J., & Cossu, G. (1991). Poor readers and black swans. *Mind and Language, 2,* 135–139.

Martinez, M., Roser, N., Worthy, J., Strecker, S., & Gough, P. (1997). Children libraries and children's book selections: Redefining "access" in self-selected reading. In C. Kinzer, K. Hinchman, & D. Leu (Eds.), *Inquiries in literacy theory and practice: Forty-sixth yearbook of the National Reading Conference* (pp. 265–272). Chicago: National Reading Conference.

Masonheimer, P., Drum, P., & Ehri, L. (1984). Does environmental print identification lead children into word reading? *Journal of Reading Behavior, 16,* 257–271.

Massaro, D., & Sanocki, T. (1993). Visual information processing in reading. In D. Willows, R. Kruk, & E. Corcos (Eds.), *Visual processes in reading and reading disabilities,* (pp. 139–161). Hillsdale, NJ: Lawrence Erlbaum Associates.

Mayer, S. (1997). *What money can't buy: Family income and children's life chances.* Cambridge, MA: Harvard University Press.

McBride-Chang, C., Manis, F., Seidenberg, M., Custodio, R., & Doi, L. (1993). Print exposure as a predictor of word reading and reading comprehension in disabled and nondisabled readers. *Journal of Educational Psychology, 85,* 230–238.

McGee, L. (1986). Young children's environmental print reading. *Childhood Education, 63,* 118–125.

McGee, L., & Lomax, R. (1990). On combining apples and oranges: A response to Stahl and Miller. *Review of Educational Research, 60,* 133-140.

McGee, L., Lomax, R., & Head, M. (1988). Young children's written language knowledge: What environmental and functional print reading reveals. *Journal of Reading Behavior, 20,* 99–118.

McGuinness, D. (1997). *Why our children can't read and what we can do about it: A scientific revolution in reading.* New York: The Free Press.

McKenna, M., Stratton, B., Grindler, M., & Jenkins, S. (1995). Differential effects of whole language and traditional instruction on reading attitudes. *Journal of Reading Behavior, 27,* 19–44.

McLaughlin, B. (1978). The monitor model: Some methodological considerations. *Language Learning, 28,* 309–322.

McQuillan, J. (1996a). SAT Verbal scores and the library: Predicting high school reading achievement in the United States. *Indiana Media Journal, 18*(3), 65–70.

McQuillan, J. (1996b, August). *The effects of print access on reading acquisition.* Poster session presented at the 1996 Whole Language Umbrella, St. Paul, Minnesota.

McQuillan, J. (1997a). *Access to print and formal instruction in reading acquisition.* Unpublished Ph.D. dissertation, Los Angeles: University of Southern California.

McQuillan, J. (1997b). The effect of incentives on reading. *Reading Research and Instruction, 36,* 111–125.

McQuillan, J. (in press-a). Is learning to read outside of school without formal instruction common? *Journal of Reading Education.*

McQuillan, J. (in press-b). The case of late readers. In P. Dryer (Ed.), *The 61st Annual Claremont Reading Conference Yearbook.* Claremont, CA: Claremont Reading Conference.

McQuillan, J. (in press-c). The use of free voluntary reading in heritage language programs: A review of research. In S. Krashen, L. Tse, & J. McQuillan (Eds.), *Heritage language development.* Culver City, CA: Language Education Associates.

McQuillan, J. (in press-d). The rhetoric and reality of California's reading situation. In C. Weaver (Ed.), *Reconsidering a balanced approach to reading.* Urbana, IL: National Council of Teachers of English.

Mervar, K., & Hiebert, E. (1989). Literature selection strategies and amount of reading in two literacy approaches. In S. McCormick & J. Zutell (Eds.), *Cognitive and social perspectives in literacy research and instruction: Thirty-eighth yearbook of the National Reading Conference* (pp. 529-535). Chicago: National Reading Conference.

Molfese, V., DiLalla, L., & Bunce, D. (1997). Prediction of the intelligence test scores of 3- to 8-year-old children by home environment, socioeconomic status, and biomedical risks. *Merrill-Palmer Quarterly, 43*(2), 219–234.

Morgan, F. (1990). *State profiles of public elementary and secondary education, 1987–1988.* Washington D.C.: Office of Educational Research and Improvement, U.S. Department of Education.

Morrison, C., Harris, A., & Auerbach, I. (1971). The reading performance of disadvantaged early and non-early readers from grades 1 through 3. *Journal of Educational Research, 65,* 23–26.

Morrow, L. (1983). Home and school correlates of early interest in literature. *Journal of Educational Research, 76,* 221–230.

Morrow, L. (1992). The impact of a literature-based program on literacy achievement, use of literature, and attitudes of children from minority backgrounds. *Reading Research Quarterly, 27,* 250–275.

Morrow, L., O'Connor, E., & Smith, J. (1990). Effects of a story reading program on the literacy development of at-risk kindergarten children. *Journal of Reading Behavior, 22,* 255–275.

Moustafa, M. (1995). Children's productive phonological recoding. *Reading Research Quarterly, 30,* 464–476.

Moustafa, M. (1997). *Beyond traditional phonics: Research discoveries and reading instruction.* Portsmouth, NH: Heinemann.

Murray, C., & Herrnstein, R. (1992). What's really behind the SAT-score decline? *The Public Interest, 106,* 32–56.

Nagy, W., Herman, P., & Anderson, R. (1985). Learning words from context. *Reading Research Quarterly, 20,* 233–253.

National Center for Educational Statistics (NCES) (1994). *Data compendium for the NAEP 1992 Reading Assessment of the nation and the states.* Washington, D.C.: U.S. Department of Education.

National Center for Educational Statistics (NCES). (1995). *Public libraries in the United States: 1993.* Washington, D.C.: U.S. Department of Education.

Newport, E., Gleitman, H., & Gleitman, L. (1977). Mother, I'd rather do it myself: Some effects and non-effects of maternal speech style. In C. Snow & C. Ferguson (Eds.), *Talking to children: Language input and acquisition* (pp. 109–149). London: Longman.

Norris, D. (1987). Strategic control of sentence context effects in a naming task. *Quarterly Journal of Experimental Psychology, 39A,* 253–275.

Okagaki, L., Frensch, P., & Gordon, E. (1995). Encouraging school achievement among Latino adolescents: Prevalence, attitudes, and school performance. *Hispanic Journal of Behavioral Sciences, 17*(2), 160–179.

Organization for Economic Cooperation and Development (OECD). (1995). *Education at a glance: OECD indicators.* Paris: Author.

Ortiz, V. (1986). Reading activities and reading proficiency among Hispanic, Black, and White students. *American Journal of Education, 95,* 59–76.

Orton Dyslexia Society. (1997). *Informed instruction for reading success: Foundations for teacher preparation.* Baltimore: Author.

Perfetti, C., Goldman, S., & Hogaboam, T. (1979). Reading skill and the identification of words in discourse context. *Memory and Cognition, 7,* 273–282.

Phillips, G., & McNaughton, S. (1990). The practice of storybook reading to preschool children in mainstream New Zealand families. *Reading Research Quarterly, 25,* 196–212.

Pinker, S. (1994). *The language instinct: How the mind creates language.* New York: William Morrow & Company.

Pinnell, G., Lyons, C., Deford, D., Bryk, A., & Seltzer, M. (1994). Comparing instructional models for literacy education of high risk first graders. *Reading Research Quarterly, 29,* 8–39.

Plessas, G., & Oakes, C. (1964). Prereading experiences of selected early readers. *Reading Teacher, 17,* 241–245.

Podolsky, A. (1991). *Public libraries in 50 states and the District of Columbia: 1989.* Washington D.C.: Office of Educational Research and Improvement, U.S. Department of Education.

Pucci, S. (1994). Supporting Spanish language literacy: Latino children and free reading resources in schools. *Bilingual Research Journal, 18,* 67–82.

Pucci, S., & Ulanoff, S. (1996). Where are the books? *CATESOL Journal, 9,* 111–115.

Purcell-Gates, V., McIntyre, E., & Freppon, P. (1995). Learning written storybook language in school: A comparison of low-SES children in skills-based and whole language classrooms. *American Educational Research Journal, 32,* 659–685.

Purves, A., & Elley, W. (1994). The role of the home and student differences in reading performance. In W. Elley (Ed.), *The IEA study of reading literacy: Achievement and instruction in thirty-two school systems* (pp. 89–122). Oxford, England: Pergamon.

Ramos, F., & Krashen, S. (in press). The impact of one trip to the public library: Making books available may be the best incentive for reading. *The Reading Teacher.*

Raz, I., & Bryant, P. (1990). Social background, phonological awareness, and children's reading. *British Journal of Developmental Psychology, 8,* 209–225.

Rodrigo, V., McQuillan, J., & Krashen, S. (1996). Free voluntary reading and vocabulary knowledge in native speakers of Spanish. *Perceptual and Motor Skills, 83,* 648–650.

Rothstein, R. (1997). *What do we know about declining (or rising) student achievement?* Arlington, VA: Educational Research Services.

Rowe, K. (1991). The influence of reading activity at home on students' attitudes towards reading, classroom attentiveness and reading achievement: An application of structural equation modeling. *British Journal of Educational Psychology, 61,* 19–35.

Rowe, K. (1997). Factors affecting students' progress in reading: Key findings from a longitudinal study. In S. Swartz & A. Klein (Eds.), *Research in reading recovery*, (pp. 53–101). Portsmouth, NH: Heinemann.

Rucker, B. (1982). Magazines and teenage reading skills: Two controlled field experiments. *Journalism Quarterly, 59*, 28–33.

Samuels, S.J. (1967). Attentional process in reading: The effect of pictures on the acquisition of reading responses. *Journal of Educational Psychology, 58*, 337–342.

Sanocki, T., & Oden, G. (1984). Contextual validity and the effects of low-constraint sentence contexts on lexical decisions. *Quarterly Journal of Experimental Psychology, 36A*, 145–156.

Sanocki, T., Goldman, K., Waltz, J., Cook, C., Epstein, W., & Oden, G. (1985). Interaction of stimulus and contextual information during reading: Identifying words within sentences. *Memory and Cognition, 13*, 145–157.

Schickedanz, J. (1990) The jury is still out on the effects of whole language and language experience approaches for beginning reading: A critique of Stahl and Miller's study. *Review of Educational Research, 60*, 127–131.

Schmittroth, L. (1994). *Statistical record of children*. Detroit: Gale Research.

Schwantes, F., Boesl, S., & Ritz, E. (1980). Children's use of context in word recognition: A psycholinguistic guessing game. *Child Development, 51*, 730–736.

Scott, J., & Ehri, L. (1990). Sight word reading in prereaders; Use of logographic vs. alphabetic access routes. *Journal of Reading Behavior, 22*, 149–166.

Seymour, P., & Elder, L. (1986). Beginning reading without phonology. *Cognitive Neuropsychology, 3*(1), 1–36.

Share, D. (1995). Phonological recoding and self-teaching: Sine qua non of reading acquisition. *Cognition, 55*, 151–218.

Shaywitz, B., Fletcher, J., Holahan, J., & Shaywitz, S. (1992). Discrepancy compared to low achievement definitions of reading disability: Results from the Connecticut Longitudinal Study. *Journal of Learning Disabilities, 25*, 639–648.

Shaywitz, B., Holford, T., Holahan, J., Fletcher, J., Stuebing, K., Francis, D., & Shaywitz, S. (1995). A Matthews effect for IQ but not for reading: Results from a longitudinal study. *Reading Research Quarterly, 30*, 894–906.

Shaywitz, B., Shaywitz, S., Fletcher, J., Pugh, K., Gore, J., Constable, T., Fulbright, R., Skudlarksi, P., Liberman, A., Shankweiler, D., Katz, L., Bronen, R., Marchione, K., Holahan, J., Francis, D., Klorman, R., Aram, D., Blachman, B., Stuebing, K., & Lacadie, C. (1996, March). *The Yale Center for the Study of Learning and Attention: Longitudinal and neurobiological studies*. Dallas, Texas: Paper presented at the Annual Meeting of the LDA.

Shaywitz, S., Shaywitz, B., Fletcher, J., & Escobar, M. (1990). Prevalence of reading disability in boys and girls: Results of the Connecticut Longitudinal Study. *Journal of the American Medical Association, 264*(8), 998–1002.

Shaywitz, S., Escobar, M., Shaywitz, B., Fletcher, J., & Makuch, R. (1992). Evidence that dyslexia may represent the lower tail of a normal distribution of reading ability. *The New England Journal of Medicine, 326*(3), 145–150.

Shaywitz, S., Fletcher, J., & Shaywitz, B. (1994). Issues in the definition and classification of attention deficit disorder. *Topics in Language Disorders, 14*(4), 1–25.

Smith, C., Constantino, B., & Krashen, S. (1996). Differences in print environment for children in Beverly Hills, Compton, and Watts. *Emergency Librarian, 24*, 8–9.

Smith, F. (1973). *Psycholinguistics and reading*. New York: Holt, Rinehart and Winston.

Smith, F. (1983). *Essays into literacy*. Portsmouth, NH: Heinemann.

Smith, F. (1994). *Understanding reading*, 5th edition. Hillsdale, NJ: Lawrence Erlbaum Associates.

Smith, M.C. (1993). Change in reading ability and attitudes from childhood to adulthood: A life span perspective. In S. Yussen & M. C. Smith (Eds.), *Reading across the life span* (pp. 273–393). New York: Springer-Verlag.

Smith, M.C. (1995). Differences in adults' reading practices and literacy preferences. *Reading Research Quarterly, 31,* 196–219.

Smolkin, L., Conlon, A., & Yaden, D. (1988). Print salient illustrations in children's picture books: The emergence of written language awareness. In J. Readence & R. S. Baldwin (Eds.), *Thirty-seventh yearbook of the National Reading Conference* (pp. 58–68). Chicago: National Reading Conference.

Snow, C. (1983). Literacy and language: Relationships during the preschool years. *Harvard Educational Review, 53,* 165–189.

Snow, C., & Goldfield, A. (1982). Building stories: The emergence of information structures from conversation. In D. Tannen (Ed.), *Analyzing discourse: Text and talk* (pp. 127–141). Washington, D.C.: Georgetown University Press.

Snow, C., & Goldfield, A. (1983). Turn the page please: Situation specific language learning. *Journal of Child Language, 10,* 551–570.

Snow, C., & Ninio, A. (1986). The contracts of literacy: What children learn from learning to read books. In W. Teale & E. Sulzby (Eds.), *Emergent literacy* (pp. 116–138). Norwood, NJ: Ablex.

Snyder, T., & Hoffman, C. (1995). *Digest of education statistics, 1995.* Washington, D.C.: U.S. Department of Education.

Sowell, T. (1997, August 3). What money can't buy: Which comes first, the destructive behavior or the poverty? *Orange County Register,* C3.

Stahl, S., & Miller, P. (1989). Whole language and language experience approaches for beginning reading: A quantitative research synthesis. *Review of Educational Research, 59,* 87–116.

Stahl, S., & Murray, B. (1993). Environmental print, phonemic awareness, letter recognition, and word recognition. In D. Leu, C. Kinzer, L. Ayre, J. Peter, & S. Bennett, (Eds.), *Examining central issues in literacy research, theory, and practice: Forty-second yearbook of the National Reading Conference* (pp. 227–233). Chicago: National Reading Conference.

Stahl, S., McKenna, M., & Pagnucco, J. (1994). The effects of whole language instruction: An update and reappraisal. *Educational Psychologist, 29,* 175–185.

Stanovich, K. (1982). Individual differences in cognitive processes of reading: II. Text-level process. *Journal of Learning Disabilities, 15*(9), 549–554.

Stanovich, K. (1986). Mathew effects in reading: Some consequences of individual differences in the acquisition of literacy. *Reading Research Quarterly, 21*(4), 360–406.

Stanovich, K. (1992). Speculations on the causes and consequences of individual differences in early reading acquisition. In P. Gough, L. Ehri, & R. Treiman (Eds.), *Reading acquisition* (pp. 307–342). Hillsdale, NJ: Lawrence Erlbaum Associates.

Stanovich, K. (1993). The language code: Issues in word recognition. In S. Yussen and M. C. Smith (Eds.), *Reading across the life span* (pp. 111–135). New York: Springer-Verlag.

Stanovich, K., & Cunningham, A. (1992). Studying the consequences of literacy within a literate society: The cognitive correlates of print exposure. *Memory and Cognition, 20,* 51–68.

Stanovich, K., & Cunningham, A. (1993). Where does knowledge come from? Specific associations between print exposure and information acquisition. *Journal of Educational Psychology, 85,* 211–229.

Stanovich, K., & Stanovich, P. (1995). How research might inform the debate about early reading acquisition. *Journal of Research in Reading, 18,* 87–105.

Stanovich, K., & West, R. (1983). On priming by a sentence context. *Journal of Experimental Psychology: General, 112,* 1–36.

Stanovich, K., & West, R. (1989). Exposure to print and orthographic processing. *Reading Research Quarterly, 24,* 402–433.

Stanovich, K., Cunningham, A., & Feeman, D. (1984). Relationship between early reading acquisition and word decoding with and without context: A longitudinal study of first grade children. *Journal of Educational Psychology, 76,* 668–677.

Stanovich, K., West, R., & Harrison, M. (1995). Knowledge growth and maintenance across the life span: The role of print exposure. *Developmental Psychology, 31,* 811–826.

Stedman, L. (1996). As assessment of literacy trends, past and present. *Research in the Teaching of English, 30,* 283–302.

Stedman, L. (1997). International achievement differences: An assessment of the new perspective. *Educational Researcher, 26*(3), 4–15.

Stewart, J. (1996). The blackboard bungle: California's failed reading experiment. *LA Weekly, 18*(14), 22–29.

Stothard, S., & Hulme, C. (1996). A comparison of reading comprehension and decoding difficulties in children. In C. Cornoldi & J. Oakhill (Eds.), *Reading comprehension difficulties: Processes and interventions* (pp. 93–112). Mahwah, NJ: Lawrence Erlbaum Associates.

Stuart, M., & Coltheart, M. (1986). Does reading develop in a series of stages? *Cognition, 30,* 139–181.

Sutton, M. (1969). Children who learned to read in kindergarten: A longitudinal study. *Reading Teacher, 22,* 595–683.

Swaffer, J., & Woodruff, M. (1978). Language for comprehension: Focus on reading. *Modern Language Journal, 5,* 27–32.

Symons, S., Szuszkiewicz, T., & Bonnell, C. (1996). Parental print exposure and young children's language and literacy skills. *The Alberta Journal of Educational Research, 42,* 49–58.

Taylor, B., Frye, B., & Maruyama, G. (1990). Time spent reading and reading growth. *American Educational Research Journal, 27,* 351–362.

Taylor, D., & Dorsey-Gaines, C. (1983). *Growing up literate: Learning from inner-city families.* Portsmouth, NH: Heinemann.

Teale, W. (1978). Positive environments for learning to read: What studies of early readers tell us. *Language Arts, 55,* 922–932.

Tobin, A. W., & Pikulski, J. J. (1988). A longitudinal study of the reading achievement of early and non-early readers through sixth grade. In J. Readence and R. S. Baldwin (Eds.), *Dialogues in literacy research: Thirty-seventh Yearbook of the National Reading Conference* (pp. 49-58). Chicago: National Reading Conference.

Torgesen, J. & Hecht, S. (1996). Preventing and remediating reading disabilities: Instructional variables that make a special difference for special students. In M. Graves, P. Van Den Broek, & B. Taylor (Eds.), *The First R: Every child's right to read.* New York: Teacher's College Press.

Torrey, J. (1969). Learning to read without a teacher: A case study. *Elementary English, 46,* 550–556.

Torrey, J. (1979). Reading that comes naturally: The early reader. In G. Waller & G. Mackinnon (Eds.), *Reading research: Advances in theory and practice,* Vol. 1 (pp. 1–30). New York: Academic Press.

Van Patten, B. (1987). How juries get hung: Problems with the evidence for focus on form in teaching. *Language Learning, 38,* 243–260.

Vellutino, F., Scanlon, D., Sipay, E., Small, S., Pratt, A., Chen, R., & Denkla, M. (1996). Cognitive profiles of difficult-to-remediate and readily remediated poor readers: Early intervention as a vehicle for distinguishing between cognitive and experiential deficits as basic causes of specific reading disability. *Journal of Educational Psychology, 88,* 601–638.

Wagner, R., & Stanovich, K. (1996). Expertise in reading. In K.A. Ericcson (Ed.), *The road to excellence* (pp. 189–226). Mahwah, NJ: Lawrence Erlbaum Associates.

Walberg, H. (1996). U.S. schools teach reading least productively. *Research in the Teaching of English, 30,* 328–343.

Weaver, C. (1994). *Reading process and practice,* 2nd edition. Portsmouth, NH: Heinemann.

West, R., & Stanovich, K. (1978). Automatic contextual facilitation in readers of three ages. *Child Development, 49,* 717–727.

West, R., Stanovich, K., & Mitchell, H. (1993). Reading in the real world and its correlates. *Reading Research Quarterly, 28,* 34–50.

White, H. (1990). School library collections and services: Ranking the states. *School Library Media Quarterly, 19,* 13–26.

White, K. (1983). The relation between socioeconomic status and academic achievement. *Psychological Bulletin, 91,* 461–481.

Wolf, F. (1986). *Meta-analysis.* Beverly Hills, CA: Sage Publications.

Woodcock, R., & Johnson, M. B. (1977). *Woodcock-Johnson Psycho-Educational Battery: Examiner's Manual.* Allen, TX: DLM Teaching Resources.

Worthy, J. (1996). Removing barriers to voluntary reading for reluctant readers: The role of school and classroom libraries. *Language Arts, 73,* 483–492.

Yaden, D. (1984). Reading research in metalinguistic awareness: Findings, problems, and classroom applications. *Visible Language, 18,* 5–47.

Yaden, D. (1988). Understanding stories through repeated read-alouds: How many does it take? *Reading Teacher, 41,* 556–560.

Yaden, D., Smolkin, L., & Conlon, A. (1989). Preschoolers' questions about pictures, print conventions, and story text during reading aloud at home. *Reading Research Quarterly, 24,* 188–214.

Yopp, H. (1988). The validity and reliability of phonemic awareness tests. *Reading Research Quarterly, 23,* 159–177.

Index

111